EMPATHY IMPACT

THE WILD EFFECTS OF KINDNESS IN ACTION

KIM BERRY JONES   SIERRA BAILEY   MICHELLE MERRITT
SHAY MICHELLE DRAPEAU   SARAH SOUCIE EYBERG
SANDY STEWART   DEBRA BLUE   DAYNE WHITEHURST
AVERY TOOMES   LURLEEN LADD   CIJI WAGNER
ANA RUELAS   HILARY GRAHAM   ALICIA RAFFKIND
DANYELE EASTERHAUS

SULIT
PRESS

CONTENTS

ABOUT SULIT PRESS

Sulit Press is a boutique publishing house that provides high-touch support to thought leaders, industry shakers, and changemakers writing impactful nonfiction. Whether you're publishing a personal memoir, an industry-specific solo book, or contributing to a collaborative multi-author book, we help you go from aspiring author to published author—with clarity, confidence, and community.

Founder and CEO Michelle Savage is an international best-selling author, speaker, and mentor who helps high-vibe, heart-centered women share and amplify their stories. With a background in publishing, coaching, and storytelling, Michelle is passionate about helping women turn their lived experience into professional assets—whether that means a book, a brand, or a bigger platform.

She's led women through their first published pieces, hosted sold-out retreats, and built a thriving community of bold, generous authors who are ready to be seen.

Want to learn more?

Visit www.sulitpress.com

INTRODUCTION

"Could a greater miracle take place than for us to look through each other's eyes for an instant?"

— Henry David Thoreau

Empathy is easy to say but harder to live. It asks us to pause, and to listen, and to stay soft in a world that rewards sharpness.

It is more than imagining ourselves in someone else's place. It is forgiveness when the wound still stings, compassion that reaches beyond misunderstanding, and love that does not measure or withhold.

For the women in these pages, empathy has taken many forms. It has appeared in moments of care, in leadership that listens, in the courage to repair what was broken, and in the decision to love again after deep loss. It has been learned through family, through work, through friendship, and through the steady act of forgiving oneself. In every story, empathy is both the teacher and the lesson.

These stories remind us that empathy cannot be taught in theory or practiced only in moments of ease. It is something we learn through living, through trial and tenderness, and through staying present when it would be easier to turn away. It asks us to slow down, to choose connection over being right, and to remember that we never truly know what someone else is carrying.

In a time when noise often replaces understanding, empathy becomes the balm. And with so much in the world to resist or be *against*, choosing to be *for* something is its own powerful revolution.

At work, at home, toward others, and toward ourselves, empathy is what brings us back to one another. It is how we mend, how we soften, and how we rise. Love, in all its forms, is the best way to witness and express the wild effects of kindness in action.

1

LOVE NEVER DIES

BY KIM BERRY JONES

*W*hen I opened the back door into the garage, the smell of rotting food hit me like a wave. Six weeks ago, Nancy left her home, walked across the street to my house, and never came back. A narrow pathway led to her kitchen, and piled around me were boxes, kitchen appliances, books, tools, and paper—paper everywhere. I walked through the kitchen and dining room, and when I reached the front room, the path ended. The only way through meant walking on squishy bags filled with stuff, pushed down enough to allow me passage through a cave of books and clothes, dimly lit by fluorescent light. My daughter, Brooke, the only one who'd been in the house before today, led me toward Nancy's bedroom.

Feeling the undertow of shock at facing what I had known about her but never seen, I was unsteady on my feet. I wished I shared Brooke or Nancy's diminutive stature to navigate this maze as I entered her bedroom. To the left in front of me was a tiny bed, nearly as small as a crib, the only place in the house where you could tell Nancy had spent time. And to my astonishment, all around the bed, taped to the walls, were twenty-five years of pictures of my children. It was then that I felt the full weight of it all—her death—her life—and her love.

As I stood in Nancy's bedroom, surrounded by decades of Christmas cards and photos of her with the kids, the memories flooded back. Over the past few weeks of Nancy's brief illness, Brooke ventured in to retrieve things that Nancy said she needed. Her father's bar mitzvah ring, a bill she hadn't paid, the emeralds she had spilled under her bed—all treasures she wanted to fill her new space, a hospital bed in my home, where she would die.

Nancy was gone now, but she was about to change my life. Actually, she was changing it all along. I just didn't realize it. So much of what I saw over the years, I had misunderstood.

Small in stature, her personality stood much taller than she did, with her eclectic choice of clothing, a visor that always matched her outfit, glasses repaired with tape, and her keys hanging on a chain around her neck. Our neighbor for thirty years, we'd shared thousands of moments—too many times when I wished her daily visits were shorter, and once when we didn't speak for six months.

Over the years, we had piled moments on top of each other, some of them raw and messy, but many full of laughter, happiness, and beauty. Those moments wove together and built a connection that allowed her to invite me into her death. It was an unconditional love reciprocated as we stumbled through life together.

Just weeks earlier, I pulled up to my house after another soul-crushing day at work. Nancy sat in her chair on my front porch, using my Wi-Fi again after her fight with the internet company led her to cancel hers. Weary frustration washed over me, and I knew I would not make it through my front door without a conversation.

Not today, Nancy, I thought as I walked towards my front door. *I have nothing left. If you follow me through the door, how will I collapse on the couch and catch my breath?* Sucking down my fatigue, I greeted her as I turned the lock to the door, and I noticed she did not look right. Her skin was the color of a lemon that was too old to eat, withered and dark yellow. Why was I just noticing this?

"Nancy, what is going on?" I asked. "You do not look good." As we talked, she admitted to some strange symptoms over the past few days. We were emerging from the pandemic, and I knew from years of observation that Nancy did not have a doctor and would never seek medical care, no matter her ailment. "Please let me take you to the hospital, Nancy," I said, afraid for her now.

"I will only go if you promise to stay with me the entire time," she finally relented. I rushed her to my car, only to have the nurse turn me away at the door because of Covid restrictions. Early the next morning, as the sun peeked above the eastern horizon, Nancy called to tell me her body was filled with cancer, attacking her liver and ovaries with no hope for treatment.

The six weeks that followed were both the longest and shortest of my life. We brought her back from the hospital to her new home, my living room couch. A few days in, I'd moved her from the living room to her own room, partly for her comfort and partly for my own sanity. She held court in the middle of the action, my friend who'd lived a solitary life, now the center of attention. My husband, Chris, and I never had a conversation about whether we should take Nancy into our home. This was not because we are heroes or saints, but because of something unspoken that compelled us. There would be no other path.

My daughter-in-law, Sydney, once asked my son, Zach, what some of his favorite memories of Nancy were. "I can't tell you one," he answered. "She is in all my memories." That was spot on, because Nancy was almost always around, peering in through our large front window or tapping quietly to get my attention in case one of the kids was still napping. Sometimes she would stand in the kitchen, refusing to take a seat at the table while the rest of us ate dinner. Or she would sit on the floor at the foot of the couch, providing a rundown of the state of the union.

For every one of my kids' birthday parties, Nancy was by my side, pouring her love of crafting and baking into the day. For Brooke's princess party, Nancy dug the "cake Barbie" from her stash—the naked doll you could stick into the top of a cake—and baked it in a giant measuring cup to look like a skirt, decorated in pink and purple frosting. At the party, she navigated between two princess stations, one painting tiny five-year-old nails and the other stringing beads for tiny bracelets. She even loaned me a peach flowing gown so I could be the "Mama Princess" of the party.

My kids did not know life without Nancy. As their only babysitter, she had filled the house with Barbies, books, and Matchbox cars. She'd led countless craft projects, organized a thousand Barbie outfits, helped Zach outfit his army outpost in the backyard, and given me a lifetime of both welcome and unsolicited advice. She was there when I was home alone with the kids and cut my foot open on broken glass. She held onto Brooke when I rushed to the hospital in an ambulance after Zach cracked his head on the cement. Just the day before we began our journey to the end of her life, she was lugging bricks into Chris's truck, helping him finish a home construction project.

When morning sickness confined me to the couch with two-year-old Zach watching *Bear in the Big Blue House* on repeat, Nancy was there with ginger to quiet my stomach. Every Saturday afternoon, she arrived from her garage-sale hunt or a library-book sale with stacks of books for the kids. For nine months, she held Brooke every evening so I could make dinner. She was the only one whom Brooke would willingly go to besides me.

Mixed in between these moments of grace were times when I dreaded her visit, training my five- and two-year-olds to "hit the deck" when we saw her coming, lying flat on the ground in the back room where she couldn't see us through the window. There were days when I left the "Quiet, Naptime" sign hanging on the front door for just a little longer. One time, she hurt my tender mother's heart so severely with her criticism of my parenting that we circled each other in silence for six months before I caved and called her back into our yard. During these years, I did not understand that every day for her was filled with anticipation of time spent with me. Many days, my heart was too clouded to see her at all.

We had lived a lifetime with her, but in so many ways, I missed what was happening. I did not see through her quips about my kids, and my boundaries were too unformed; my sense of self was often too fragile to understand that she was much more than an eccentric woman who hung out at my house too much. I did not always understand that her love for my family was driven by her love for me, the daughter she never had. I could not yet see that she would hand me the seeds to grow something that she would not be here to experience.

Now here we were, Nancy facing a cancer diagnosis and both of us facing what we knew would be a brief and uncertain period. Our lives had merged completely. I now found myself responsible for finding things she could eat, monitoring her bowels, coordinating with nurses, and untangling her complicated relationship with details so that she could have some of her affairs in order before she died.

In the first week of her stay at our home, Nancy decided to go through one of the countless bags of papers she kept—half a dozen of these bags were piled around her as she spent her days in the hospital bed. As I helped her decide which scraps of paper to keep (95%) and which to toss, I found an old postcard advertisement from a plumber. On the back was my grandmother's handwriting—the recipe for her brown bread. More scraps emerged from the bag with more recipes. Nancy practically levitated with the delight of proving to me, once again, that my trash was her treasure—and now it was mine, too. Years before, so long ago that I had no memory of it, I had thrown out a recipe box, deciding that the scraps were not important. Now, with two decades of my grandmother's absence, this trash was an heirloom. I had thrown it away, and Nancy had rescued it for me, knowing that someday I would need it.

During those six weeks, we never knew what was coming next. Yet my exhaustion and her pain were somehow covered in an unmistakable grace, and we lived hour by hour trying to absorb the new reality. Two weeks in, Nancy was hospitalized again, and I was attempting to work from her hospital room. My cell phone rang with a reporter calling to interview me about human trafficking, an expertise I had acquired over ten years of building a nonprofit organization. Instead of taking the call in the hallway, she encouraged me to stay put while I answered the reporter's questions. As I hung up, Nancy exclaimed, "You little brat. I had no idea you were that smart."

Here was our dynamic in focus. Her words were not softened, and my receipt of them was not smooth. I took in her delight with confusion and left for a work meeting I couldn't avoid. Upon my return, her enthusiasm had not dimmed, and when I tried to tell her about the success of my meeting, I was met with, "Shut up and sit down. I have something to tell you."

In the two hours I had been gone, Nancy had called her sister, her only living relative, and hatched a plan. There in the hospital, with IV antibiotics fighting an infection in her blood and an external drain attached to her liver, Nancy set her legacy in motion. Thirty years into our friendship, I learned something about her I had not known. She had money. A lot of it, and she had decided what to do with it. She wanted to create the Nancy Neffson and Wetmore Family Foundation, and she wanted me to lead it.

Dumbfounded and in disbelief, I stumbled from the hospital room and called Chris from the car to try to explain what had transpired. Mainly, I could not grasp what it meant. All I could think about was that my friend was dying, and I felt totally unequipped to handle any of it.

When Nancy was able to return to our home a week later, our entire focus was on keeping her out of pain and navigating hospice. Nurses were in and out of my house on twelve-hour shifts, and I was managing Nancy's reaction to each one of them. "Nurse Ratched" had to go after two visits—two visits too many for Nancy, who would not be managed. We settled on one particularly kind nurse who modified her schedule to accommodate us as much as possible. At the beginning of her journey, an appointment with the oncologist had been scheduled for four weeks out. Nancy hung on that date, counting on answers that might help her beat the cancer, while at the same time, reminding us she just wanted a few more good weeks. Now, just two weeks before she died, I arranged for the oncologist to talk to Nancy by phone, and he let her know the cancer was too advanced to be treated. This was the last day she ate, resolved now to hasten the inevitable.

We had the hospital bed, the portable toilet, and all of the other supplies crammed into Zach's old room. One evening, a few days after she had decided she would no longer eat, Nancy summoned each family member, one at a time, into her room for a private conversation. She had something specific to tell each one of us, starting with me and Chris, who had first met her when we moved into our neighborhood as newlyweds. Next came our kids, who had never known life without Nancy, followed by our daughter-in-law, Sydney, and our daughter's fiancé, Brady, who were still adjusting to this unconventional arrangement.

I don't remember what she told me. I do remember wanting to know exactly what she had said to the others, but no one shared their sacred moment. Nancy had been working for weeks to get Zach and Sydney's miniature dachshund to warm up to her, and that evening, Juni napped on the bed beside her.

After the rounds, we all gathered around Nancy's bed, crammed into the small room that was now filled with the emotion of seven people all coming to terms with the same reality, but each one doing it alone.

Looking around the room, Nancy smiled and said, "It doesn't get any better than this."

What?

My body was weary. My brain foggy. My emotions fragmented. I was responsible for her, and I felt responsible for each member of my family, too, and their grief. I had no time to figure out what I was supposed to feel. But in that moment, something became crystal clear: this woman, whom I loved and had also found to be impossible, was content. She knew, deeply knew, that she was loved. And that was all that mattered.

In those final moments, clouded by my grief, disbelief, and exhaustion, I didn't yet have the clarity to see that she had kept her true self to the tiny circle of our family. Nancy was not someone that most people knew. She loved to greet people as they walked by her house with their dogs, commenting on the iron dog statue, Ruff, that she kept in the yard. She attended the neighborhood women's monthly meetings, but only one of them came to see her while she was sick. As her life wound down to hours, we tucked in as a family and held a quiet and solitary vigil—just us.

A few days later, on a bright fall Sunday morning, Nancy fell into a sleep and slipped away—choosing her moment in the brief space between my bedside vigil and my visit to the bathroom.

In the last days of her life, she had solicited a promise from her sister, Diane. Nancy was short on details, like she always had been when it came to business matters. Diane, on the other hand, was long on follow-through, a role she had played all of Nancy's life. She drew up the papers—the will and trust that had not existed mere weeks earlier. Nancy would sign them with the last shaky movements of her hand. The foundation would happen.

Two years later, I walked my own cancer journey and a brush with death, which, fortunately, she did not have to witness. Facing my own mortality gave me the clarity I needed to set down my nonprofit work and jump into creating the foundation. The Kinship Fund, an initiative of the Nancy Neffson and Wetmore Family Foundation, is Nancy's legacy. It grows from the last wishes of a woman who took a considerable risk on me to create something she could just barely imagine.

Taking with me the knowledge of Nancy's feminist roots, her own experience as an outsider, and her care for those who struggled in life, the mission of the Kinship Fund focuses on women and girls, supporting programs that keep girls in school, out of juvenile detention, and provide access to help people live lives of well-being and promise.

After a decade in the nonprofit world, I finally stepped away from the cycle of proving worth. For years, I'd spoken the language foundations wanted to hear, translating heart work into metrics, stretching stories into outcomes that could fit in their boxes. Each "successful" ask came with a quiet cost—a dimming of the very spark that had drawn me to the work in the first place.

When I left, I carried with me Nancy's rebel heart, tucked like a compass in my pocket. I didn't know exactly where it would lead, only that I wanted to find a different way—one that refused to accept that power and privilege were the price of doing good.

These days, I pour my energy through a single filter that Nancy taught me: seeing people, not projects. Relationships, not transactions. Taking the time she always took with me to be present. Imagine if philanthropy itself bowed its head—approaching communities not with scrutiny, but with humility, and showing up not to dictate outcomes, but to listen, to believe, to walk alongside. What might we unlock then, if we trusted that those who carry the weight of the problem also carry the wisdom to solve it?

Nancy would have wanted me to do it this way. She didn't trust big government, business, or industry. She chose to invest her life in a select few who were willing to love her just the way she was and invited her into their messy spaces to live life. She chose us. And then she chose me to find a way forward, without her, where she could live on. Perhaps I am just the one to steward her legacy through a foundation that breaks the traditional rules. In the process, true kinship emerges, and everyone in our community has the opportunity to thrive.

One day, before she died, I sat by her bed and asked her, "Nancy, when you get wherever you are going... if there is a way for you to let me know how you are, to say hi... will you make sure you do that?"

"Well," she answered (every single answer always started with "well"). "I don't think I am going to have time for that. But if I do, I will probably come back as a cat."

On the first day back at my university office after she died, a small black cat wandered in, explored the space, and settled into a chair in my sitting area. For three days, that cat showed up every afternoon, took a nap, and left. After the third day, I never saw her again. But it taught me that I can talk to Nancy whenever I want, and I do.

"Nancy, if you were here, how would you focus on who to help?"

Sometimes I talk to her in my head as I work. There are days when I remember the ways I didn't see her while she was here. Many times, I failed to make an effort to get to know her better. I might have been too tired that day, or frustrated that she didn't seem to want to know my opinion, or wishing she would catch on and leave. Sometimes it felt like she lacked awareness of her impact on me, on us as a family. Something in my core, though, kept me continuing to open the door, pull up the chair, or set down the work and talk.

The day before Nancy slipped into an unresponsive state, she grabbed my hand and peered at me, saying, "Kim, all that time when I was at the house... I knew I was staying too long. I knew you sometimes wanted me to leave, but you needed me. Everything I have ever done for Brooke, Zach, or Chris was always for you."

She looked at me with her serious eyes. "It was always because of you."

The fragments of our lives had culminated in this pivotal moment, a fork in the road. She was leaving, and I was left. I learned more about her in this brief transition than in the six million hours we had spent together. Empathy did not mean I always felt willing or ready, but it had grown between us as we exposed our imperfections and flaws to one another. I brought this with me into a space that was clear, certain, and filled with love. It was precisely because of our flaws and imperfections that I found the strength I needed to bear witness to the sacred moments of her dying.

Unconditional love does not mean you love without error. It has nothing to do with agreeing on every issue or sharing the same background. This kind of love takes in the good days and the bad days. It contemplates the complexities and shows up anyway. Family doesn't have to come from blood, and it doesn't have to start at birth. I am reminded of Frederick Buechner, who said, "Here is the world. Beautiful and terrible things will happen. Do not be afraid." We can adopt each other at any time and choose to find one another in the beautiful and brutal moments.

The pictures surrounding her bed came down, along with everything that she loved that filled her house. This house belonged just to her, and it was where she stored all of the memories from past adventures and the parts and pieces of plans for future projects. In a final act of radical love, Nancy left her house to my husband, who lovingly restored it into a home where, someday, my grandchildren might live. And when they do, they will know all about Nancy.

As I sit at my desk each day, I can turn to look out my window and see Ruff, the iron dog, still standing under the treasured giant elm tree in her yard. And I see her there, watching me. So proud of me, and so happy to see how she lives on in the world, changing lives every day in ways she never would have imagined.

As I look out my office window, I whisper to her, *"Nancy, it's hard here without you, and I wish I could take back every time I didn't welcome you with open arms."*

"*It's okay,*" she whispers back to me through the wind in the tree. "*I knew I was loved, and the love changed all of us. And love never dies. So, get busy. We have the world to change.*"

KIM BERRY JONES

Kim Berry Jones is the President of the Kinship Fund, a private foundation that uplifts women and girls to stay in school, stay out of prison, and be rooted in possibility. Kim practices community-driven, trust-based philanthropy, building long-term partnerships that enable everyone in the community to thrive.

With C-suite experience spanning healthcare, marketing, and nonprofit leadership, Kim knows that real innovation starts with the courage to imagine new ways forward. A highlight was launching the first full-tuition college scholarship in the nation for survivors of human trafficking.

Kim's focus is on shaking up philanthropy and inspiring transformational impact as a speaker, author, and advocate.

Kim's daughter, a special education teacher, and son, a police officer, are her greatest joys. She and her husband,

Chris, live in San Diego and share the house with three dogs who also believe they have a seat at the table.

kim@kinshipfund.com
kinshipfund.com
www.linkedin.com/in/kimberryjones

2

THE FRIENDSHIP THAT BECAME A HOUSE

BY SIERRA BAILEY

"*H*ow soon can you deposit the money in my account?"

Kate's words were rushed. I was silent for a beat too long as I tried to gather my thoughts.

"Um, ah, okay," I stumbled. "Can you tell me exactly what you want to buy, and where you plan on putting it?" Kate still had six months before she moved into her new college apartment. What could she possibly need right now?

"I have a storage unit with some of Mom's stuff. I can put them in there." She took a breath. "Mom said the money would help me furnish the apartment. It's just a few things, but they're vintage, so I'm nervous they'll sell. There's a beautiful side table that's $250, and this mirror —you should see it, it's gorgeous—that's $2,000..."

My brain stopped processing when I heard $2,000. Did I hear that correctly? I was not prepared for a phone call from Kate at 9 p.m., days after her mother died, requesting money for a mirror that I knew—and she knew—that her mother would never have said yes to. I felt blindsided that this was even coming up when we were all still reeling from her death, and honestly, I was at a loss for how to respond. My face got tingly, and I wanted to throw up. I feared I wasn't prepared for anything that was to come.

Kate's mother and my dear friend, Heather, had just died from cancer. Although we knew it was coming, it felt swift, unfair, and much too soon for everyone, especially for Heather. If I felt knocked off my feet by the shock of the situation, I could only imagine how her daughters felt.

In the final months of Heather's life, she did what she felt was the only way to cope: she continued to work. Her life insurance policy was up to date; she tied up her affairs with a neat bow. She said all the things she had wanted to say to those she loved, and she did what she could to ensure her daughters would have people. As it turns out, I was one of those people.

Why was I the one receiving the phone call about the approval of the purchase of vintage mirrors? A few months prior, Heather and I took one of our usual long walks around Town Lake. These walks became slower with each passing month. Although we were two years into her diagnosis, I was just learning that the prognosis was not what I thought it was. The stage four colon cancer had now metastasized to her lungs.

Heather told me she had a big favor to ask and that I was not to answer her that day, but to talk it out with Adam, my husband, and really think about it. Heather knew me well; she knew I made decisions quickly, without regrets, and would want to reply immediately. But I also knew her well. Heather was a wonderful mix of logical and woo-woo. She had a master's in library science and practiced energy work. She was not a quick decision-maker and wanted to weigh all the information and options before taking a step. Any ask came with a lot of forethought.

The first part of the favor was that I would serve as the executor of her will, create trusts for her two daughters, Kate and Anna, who were then twenty and seventeen years old, respectively, and be their trustee for a term of fourteen years. Apart from the fact that Heather's core values were wildly different than those of her family, she explained that she had never discussed money with her family because of the complicated relationship with Kate and Anna's father. She did not want anyone else to know there were trusts, how much there was, or anything about her finances. She also wanted someone who would probably not die in the next ten years, which eliminated the grandparents due to age and health issues. I was surprised she asked this of me, but I understood why I was chosen. From a logistical and financial point of view, it made sense.

But the second part felt different. She explained that she really wanted me to become the person in Kate and Anna's life whom they could call when they needed a shoulder to lean on, an ear to listen, someone to talk things through with, and someone who she knew would give them good advice. She explained that I had been that person for her, and she wanted to gift them that aspect of our friendship. This meant the most to Heather.

There was one glaring issue: I am a woman who chose not to have children. I've had minimal contact with teenagers and young women beyond a few mentoring situations. I had only met her daughters once in passing. They did not know me at all. Why would she ask this of me?

But, as promised, I kept my gut reaction to myself and went home to think about it. In the days following our walk, I didn't think too much about the fact that I hardly knew her daughters—perhaps I should have, but not being around kids made me oblivious to this. Instead, I began to think a good deal about friendship. And the friendships of women as we age.

It made me think about how often we reference childhood friends, and those we carry through into adulthood, as the strong friendships in our lives. I often mourn that moving and changing schools twice disrupted the natural flow of my young friendships, leaving me without many friends from my childhood.

It made me think about how often I see in movies and books the difficulty of making friends and forming deep connections as grown-ups. But here I was, experiencing a very deep and meaningful friendship with Heather that was forged in my forties. I had only known Heather for five years before she died, which is part of why I hadn't become close with her daughters.

It made me think of the friends who had called me in a panic because they didn't have an emergency contact in Austin, and wondered if it was okay to list my name on the form they were filling out.

It made me think of my mom when I was a teenager, maybe sixteen, and the distress in her voice when she explained that if she died, there was a bank account to take care of me and my three younger sisters, the youngest of whom was not yet a year old. She gave strict advice not to let anyone separate us or take us in—that I would be fine and could do it on my own. While I question whether I'm recalling that memory correctly, it made me feel a deep empathy for Heather and her desire to choose the people who would be influential in her daughters' lives.

Obviously, I said yes.

I was fortunate to have had a few more months with Heather, during which I had the chance to hear more stories about Kate and Anna growing up, gaining a better understanding of the family dynamics and delicate relationships (or lack thereof). I asked her questions that I thought they may one day ask, and I enjoyed a little extra time with my friend as she filled me in on everything she could think to share.

Then, she was gone.

Which brings us to the morning after the phone call about the mirror. Thankfully, I was so shocked that all I could mutter at 9 p.m. was that I would call in the morning. I found myself questioning whether I was qualified for this role as I texted their grandmother. I needed to consult with an expert. Grandmothers are my favorite people. Generally, they are wise, take zero crap, and often have equally sassy friends. I never wanted to be a mom, but I've wanted to be a grandparent since I was a little kid.

We got on the phone, and I explained the 9 p.m. call. As grandmothers do, she made it all better. Apparently, what was going on was obvious: children test the boundaries to see where they are. And I was being tested. We talked it out and began one of the most delightful side effects of the whole situation: our own wonderful friendship. This was the first of many calls we regularly have to check in about Kate and Anna, and with each other.

After I hung up, I reflected on my past experiences that would help me get through this. What were my experiences with children, as a mentor or as a guide? I'm the oldest of four sisters, which means I am, although older, still an equal. My role with my nieces and nephews, as none of them live near me, is that of "Vacation Auntie" who is married to the "Fun Uncle." I buy them things, get excited about action figures and glitter, and tell them to "ask your parents" when they ask me if they're allowed to do something. I don't dare make a parenting decision, because... what do I know?

Outside of family, while building my jewelry business, I had employees and interns, people who worked for me. Through college and the early days of my business, I was a GM of a bar and then of a private club. The job also required a lot of emotion-reading with the customers. I have volunteered extensively over the years, serving on boards and as president of several nonprofit organizations, including Texas Women in Business. And, of course, years of friendships, which often include a tiny bit of hearing stories of their kids. That was the moment when I also realized: I don't hang out with many moms.

Only a few days into this new role with Kate and Anna, I felt incredibly unqualified and out of my league. The only thing I knew was that there was no turning back now, and I really didn't want one of our first conversations to be a hard *no*. I took a deep breath, told myself to stop being so dramatic, and reminded myself that her mother died less than a week ago and Kate's twenty-year-old brain was not yet fully developed.

As you can imagine, especially if you have ever interacted with young adults, this was a minor blip that was easily smoothed over and moved past. And part of why it was easy to move on was that I was not her parent. I was an adult she knew cared enough about her to step into this role, and who wanted to talk through a decision with her in a logical manner. I realized I was more prepared than I thought and that Heather knew the empathetic traits I had shown her over the years of our friendship. She knew that was the part of me that could take on this role well.

That conversation also started a shift in my thinking. The shift began with the Baader-Meinhof phenomenon, a frequency illusion in which, after becoming aware of something, you start seeing it everywhere. What I began to notice was a ton of research and commentary on forming new friendships as adults, the importance of community, and the role of women without children in society.

I've gained enough life experience to understand the power of friendship and the importance of community.

When you work on building both, the relationships can be strong enough that you feel supported not only in day-to-day companionship but also when you need it most.

There is one aspect, though, where it can be incredibly isolating: finding your people in adulthood when you don't have kids. Not having children is a decision that I have never regretted. It has enabled me to focus my time and energy on connecting, gathering, and nurturing community. But, of course, there's the other side of the coin.

Now, don't get me wrong: it's difficult for everyone to make friends as grown-ups. I noticed this especially when I moved to Austin from New York in 2011. I was in my mid-thirties, divorced, and self-employed as a jewelry designer with my own brand. I did not have children, and I was not part of a church. Although I had met my now-husband before I moved, we had just started dating, and I lived alone. My mom wisely pointed out that due to these factors, I would have to work really hard to make friends, as I would not be in any situation where I could make friends by circumstance; it was up to me to go out intentionally and find my people.

Her advice inspired me to do just that. I did things, joined things, and went to places where I hoped to meet women who also wanted to make friends. It was hard, even for someone who loves people. There were a lot of misses. Fortunately, I also have introverted tendencies that make me fine with a lot of alone time. Because there was a great deal of it. But I kept going, and I met amazing women, including Heather, whom I met at an early morning networking event. At the end of that event, I saw this woman beelining toward me from across the room. She came over and said, "The second you introduced yourself, I knew I wanted to be your friend." It was mutual.

The close friendships that are deep enough for you to ask them to watch over your children as you're dying don't come from just showing up at events and having small talk for five minutes. Experts say it takes 200 hours of quality time with someone to form a friendship. Think about how difficult it is to carve out that much time in a busy life.

It's probably why moms' groups have become so popular. Gathering with your kids once or twice a week makes those hours fly by, and friendships form fast. Unfortunately, as I am not a mom, those groups were a club that I was not qualified for. Yes, most are welcoming to all, and I have attended a few. However, the bonds between moms are potent because everyone is going through motherhood together. Without that commonality, I remained an outsider simply because I couldn't participate in most conversations.

Interestingly, as I've aged, I've noticed that friends who were once part of these mom groups feel the same sense of limbo as those of us without them, as the groups fade with time and the kids grow up, lessening the commonalities. It's similar to first friendships in school. We are friends by proximity. And those friendships often faded away as well. Friendships absolutely come and go, but those 200 hours accumulate faster when we're younger, as it's easier to spend endless hours getting to know each other when you're in the same room all day.

When I first moved to Austin, I found myself making my closest friends through networking groups. I love business, I love working, and I love talking about work. It was a great way to meet people, and most of the people closest to me were met through these groups and meet-ups.

After a few years, I found that I was making connections in wider circles and would often meet women who said they wished they had more people in their lives. I encouraged them to attend a coffee hour for one of these groups. Many pointed out that their job or business did not align with the groups, and they were right. Most networking groups are geared toward specific types of businesses or entirely exclude non-business owners or sales representatives.

Over the years, I became fascinated with learning about when and where people met their close friends. However, what I found most interesting was how many people, not just women, feel like they reach a point in life where all their friendships have faded, and the loneliness they experience can be devastating. No one seems to know where to go and find new friends. I was meeting all of these awesome women who wanted to find their people, but were struggling to figure out where to do so.

The pandemic illustrated that without in-person gatherings, loneliness skyrockets. I gave a guest lecture at the McCoy College of Business at Texas State via Zoom about small businesses, which included a section called "Making Friends as Grown-Ups." I was contacted by the school the next year, who informed me that I was the most requested returning guest lecturer, with that segment in particular often being referred to as the requested topic. Without the forced proximity of campus, students were struggling just as much as the rest of us.

I kept meeting people I wanted to connect with in low-pressure ways. Inspired by Priya Parker's book, *The Art of Gathering*, I decided to invite all the awesome women in my life to my home every other month and call it Ladies' Day, playing off how my husband, Adam, calls me *Lady*. I gathered my people; it was my day with my ladies, and it was immediately embraced by all who attended.

At one point, I asked whether it should remain bimonthly or switch to a monthly schedule. The women who were the most isolated in their work all said, "Yes, please hold it monthly." The person who requested the loudest was Heather. She was sick at this point and worked remotely; it was incredibly isolating. She loved Ladies' Day; it was her one day a month to be surrounded by a group of loud, laughing, chatty women.

Heather's last birthday was her fiftieth, and it happened to fall on a Ladies' Day. She didn't want a big fuss, but I made sure we all hugged her and celebrated her subtly, as she preferred. By the next Ladies' Day, she was gone. I hope she knew that we all cried for her that day, that the gathering of women had become her people, and that we would miss her terribly.

In the few years leading up to Heather's passing, Adam and I had experienced a lot of loss. Adam's bonus dad died of cancer. Soon after, his dad died of a different cancer. His mom died incredibly unexpectedly from a heart event. His brother, the last living nuclear family member, died a year later. Through all of this, we lost numerous friends, my cousin, my grandmother, and a dog. We were both experiencing cumulative grief, and Heather's death was at the tail end.

It was not surprising that as I was emotionally dealing with the loss of Heather, and getting used to my new role in her daughters' lives, I cried on the shoulders of the people I had intentionally spent hours with over the recent years. I began to feel a shift inside of me. It started with noticing—noticing the patterns, then asking questions, then listening. I was beginning to see the patterns that showed what was really missing, listening to what wasn't being said.

During this time, I had rented a temporary art studio as a means to move through the grief creatively. However, my rental was coming to an end, and I didn't want to move everything back home, so I began looking for a more permanent place to relocate. Unfortunately, most of the studios in Austin are either inconveniently located from my home in South Austin or used as storage and display spaces, removing the community aspect. So, I did what any delusional person on a mission does: I started looking for a building to buy that I could use for my studio and invite other artists to work in as well.

As I looked, I was doing some back-of-the-napkin calculations—figuring out how many studios there would be, who would rent them, and whether this would work —when a series of well-timed aha moments occurred. My final aha moment was in the first meeting with a bank about an SBA loan. I was informed that the U.S. Small Business Administration (SBA) does not provide loans to businesses that rent out rooms. Full stop. But their "no" made me realize that what I really wanted to create was not studio spaces. I didn't know until that moment that it wasn't about renting the rooms, but about gathering people.

I wanted to build a beautiful community center and clubhouse for South Austin. Adam, who had been part of opening two restaurants in Austin and oversaw them through the chaos of the pandemic, had taken a mental health leave when his brother died. He wanted to return to hospitality, but in a way that was not focused on food or alcohol. Because I have had eating disorders, and we have been sober for twelve years, his needs sparked something in me.

I wanted to create a space where people could work around others, rather than being closed off in offices. Equally important was that the space was not only about work. I wanted people to have a beautiful, comfortable space that felt like a home, where they could spend 200 hours with others in under a year and create real, deep, and lasting friendships as adults. And we both wanted to ensure that our members felt welcome and cared for. Where they felt nurtured, safe, and able to be vulnerable and heal if they, like us, had gone through loss. I wanted to offer events where the intention was about gathering, designed with both extroverts and introverts in mind, to facilitate connections and ensure that when people arrived, they felt like they already belonged.

This dream inspired me, and those I tapped to be involved in the project were also inspired. I gathered my team, then let my creativity fly. I've learned that as long as I'm curious and watch the patterns, I can figure it out as I go.

Maeve House has been open for almost a year. My role as CEO has continued to focus on creating a space that feels like a beautiful home away from home, as well as events that both delight our members and foster meaningful connections. Adam, as COO, is in the space during coworking hours, providing a hospitality-focused environment that makes our members excited to arrive at work. We marvel every day that when a new Maevie (what our members call themselves) walks in the door, they self-select that they belong.

We have a member, Kris, who was moving back to Austin after thirty years and intentionally chose South Austin, as she had found Maeve House online and knew that was where she would find community. She was correct. We have a member, Sarah, who moved to Austin during the pandemic and had not yet found her community. A friend of hers had stopped in for a tour and immediately told her about how she needed to pop in. Sarah walked in the door and knew she had finally found her people.

As for Kate and Anna, they do call when advice is needed! Kate lives in Austin, and we have formed such a solid monthly dinner routine that if I am late to schedule, she reaches out to make sure we see one another. Anna even humors me when she travels by emailing me copies of her itinerary, tickets, and passport. Both are strong, independent, and whip-smart women, and I love sharing the stories that their mother told me over the years, giving them glimpses into what she was like as a friend.

I am forever grateful that their presence in my life continues my connection with Heather. My friendship with Heather inspired a place where people can form their own friendships like the one we had. As long as I have my people, and they believe in me and I believe in them, I can do anything.

*The names of Heather's daughters have been changed.

SIERRA BAILEY

Sierra Bailey is an artist, writer, and entrepreneur based in Austin, Texas. She is the founder and CEO of Maeve House, a private social club for coworking and community events designed to bring people together through intentional gatherings and meaningful conversation.

A lifelong maker and storyteller, Sierra's career has spanned painting, jewelry design, authorship, and small-business leadership. Her creations and ventures have been featured in national outlets including *Elle*, *InStyle*, and *Southern Living*, as well as on *Gossip Girl* and *Criminal Minds*.

Passionate about building spaces that inspire connection, she continues to explore how art and entrepreneurship can strengthen community.

Sierra lives in Austin with her husband, Adam, and their trio of rescue dogs—including Maeve, the spirited namesake of Maeve House.

sierrabailey.com
maevehouse.com

3

THE 2.8 MILLION DOLLAR LESSON

BY MICHELLE MERRITT

*P*icture this: twenty-eight thousand crisp hundred-dollar bills stacked on a conference room table. The pile would reach your chest, so dense and heavy you'd need both hands to lift even a section of it. That's enough cash to buy a home, fund a startup, or secure a family's future. Now imagine walking past that table every day for years, leaving every single bill behind, because you didn't even know the money was yours to take.

I lost $2.8 million at the age of twenty-three and didn't even know it.

I can still feel the nausea that hit me when I finally ran the numbers years later, sitting at my desk with a calculator and years of employment records pulled up on my screen. My hands trembled as I added up what I had left on the table. Not a few thousand here and there.

Not even tens of thousands. Nearly three million dollars.

That's more money than sits in most people's entire retirement accounts. After taxes, that $2.8 million becomes $1.9 million in cold, hard cash that could have started a business, eliminated debt, or given me the kind of choices that money provides. Money that buys freedom from the 3 a.m. anxiety about making ends meet. Money that transforms "I can't afford it" into "Is this worth it to me?"

How do you lose $2.8 million without knowing it? You smile politely when they make an offer. You say, "Thank you" instead of "Let me think about it." You accept the first number because you're grateful someone wants to pay you at all. You're so naive about negotiation that you don't even realize there are ramifications to not asking for what you're worth.

The realization hit me like a physical blow. I remember putting my head down on the desk and feeling genuinely sick. All those times I'd said yes to the first offer, all those moments when I'd felt so grateful to be chosen that I forgot I had the power to choose back.

This wasn't just a financial mistake. It was a theft from my future self, committed by my naive younger self who didn't know any better. But that moment of horror, sitting at my desk staring at the evidence of my own undervaluation, didn't just make me angry. It ignited something fierce inside me.

That revelation became my declaration of war against a system that profits from people's silence about their worth. Today, as Chief Strategy Officer at D&S Executive Career Management, I've turned my $2.8 million mistake into armor for others. I refuse to let another professional walk past their own conference room table of opportunity, unaware of what's theirs for the taking. My mission is steadfast and personal: to ensure that executives, especially those who were raised to be grateful rather than strategic, learn to advocate for themselves before the regret sets in.

But the blueprint for this work didn't come from Harvard Business School or negotiation seminars. It came from two men who raised me in their living rooms and on car rides, teaching me that the most powerful negotiations happen when you can see the humanity in everyone at the table. My grandfathers understood something that most people miss entirely: empathy isn't the enemy of tough negotiation. It's the secret weapon that makes it unstoppable.

Grandfather Merritt, on my father's side, and Grandfather Minks, on my mother's side, couldn't have been more different, yet they shared an unshakable belief in fairness, respect, and human dignity. They were lifelong friends for more than forty years after their children met, each teaching me different but essential lessons about how empathy transforms the art of negotiation.

Grandfather Merritt was sharp as a tack, an insurance adjuster who could squeeze a quarter out of a nickel with barely any effort. He was a man who understood that presentation mattered, always impeccably dressed with nice hats and a love for shiny Cadillacs. But beneath his polished exterior was something deeper: he knew that respect was the foundation of any successful negotiation, and he never entered a deal without doing his homework first.

Grandfather Minks represented a different kind of strength. He worked his way through night school to become a draftsman at a foundry famous for making fire hydrants. After losing an eye in a childhood accident, he endured relentless bullying from both classmates and teachers. He worked three jobs while he and my grandmother lost three pregnancies, all while raising three children with no health insurance. Yet instead of becoming bitter, he developed an extraordinary capacity for empathy. His ability to take the hurt that caused him to be discriminated against and transform it into a relentless, unstoppable belief in family, especially me, became his greatest gift. He was my champion, offering unconditional and unending support.

What strikes me most about these two men wasn't just their individual strength, but their respect for each other and their shared commitment to treating me not as a child to be sheltered, but as a mind to be developed. From my earliest memories, they included me in discussions about world events, asked for my opinions on their projects, and treated me like the mini-adult they believed I could become. The 1970s and 1980s were a time when women had just won the right to open credit cards in their own name, and children were expected to be seen and not heard. This was the backdrop for perhaps their most empathetic act of all: giving me the space to learn, understand, and develop skills I would use for the rest of my life.

If you want to understand how to negotiate like your future depends on it, let me take you back to a small-town dealership parking lot where I watched my grandfather orchestrate what I now recognize as a master class in strategic patience.

This afternoon stands out as the moment everything clicked into place about how real negotiation works. Grandfather Merritt had found his dream car: a stunning Cadillac DeVille in a creamy color that matched expensive champagne and gleamed under the dealership lights like liquid gold. But this wasn't an impulse buy or an emotional decision. This was warfare disguised as car shopping.

True to form, he had researched everything. Not just the car's features, but the dealer's cost, their profit margins, regional pricing trends, and exactly what leverage he held as a cash buyer. He knew the salesman's quota pressures, the time of month, even the inventory turnover rate for that specific model. When Grandfather Merritt decided he wanted something, he didn't just want it; he engineered his path to getting it.

When we arrived at the dealership, he test-drove the car with the calm confidence of someone who had already won the negotiation in his mind. Satisfied that it met his standards, he approached the salesman with a check already written, announcing he was ready to buy the car. The amount on that check represented hours of research, market analysis, and strategic thinking. It wasn't a lowball offer. It was a fair price that accounted for everyone's needs while refusing to pay a penny more than necessary.

The salesman looked at the check and delivered the line that has crushed countless negotiations: "I'm sorry, Mr. Merritt, we can't sell you that car for that price."

What happened next changed how I think about power dynamics forever.

My grandfather didn't argue. He didn't get defensive or emotional. He simply smiled and said, "You absolutely can sell it for that price. I've done the research." His tone was conversational, almost friendly, as if he were discussing the weather rather than thousands of dollars.

The inevitable "let me call my manager" dance began. While we waited, I watched my grandfather examine the car again, running his hands along the champagne paint, checking the interior one more time. He wasn't anxious. He wasn't second-guessing. He had done his homework, made a fair offer, and now he was simply waiting for them to catch up to what he already knew was going to happen.

When the sales manager returned with a counteroffer that would have made most customers sign immediately, my grandfather thanked them politely and said, "I appreciate the offer, but my research shows this is the right price." He folded his check, put it back in his wallet, and headed for the door.

"Mr. Merritt, wait," the salesman called. "Let me see what else I can do."

"Call me when you're ready to accept my offer," my grandfather replied, and we left that dealership driving the same Cadillac he'd arrived in.

But here's where the story becomes legendary.

That evening, while we were washing dinner dishes and talking about everything except the car, I saw headlights pull into the driveway. Through the kitchen window, I could see that champagne-colored Cadillac under our porch light. The same salesman who had told us "no" six hours earlier was walking up to our front door, keys in hand.

"Mr. Merritt," he said when my grandfather opened the door. "If you still have that check, we'd like to make this deal work. The car is yours." He handed over the keys and a clipboard. "My manager will be here shortly to give me a ride back."

And just like that, the Cadillac, the color of pale gold with its plush interior, was sitting in his driveway.

I was fourteen years old, and I had just witnessed something that would reshape how I understood the relationship between preparation, patience, and power. This wasn't just about buying a car. It was a blueprint for every negotiation that would matter in my life.

This experience taught me foundational principles that would later revolutionize how I approach executive compensation negotiations. First, the value of research combined with respect. Second, the importance of knowing exactly what you want and being able to articulate why it's fair. Finally, and perhaps most crucially, the willingness to walk away, no matter how much your heart is set on the outcome.

But what made my grandfather's approach truly powerful wasn't just strategy. It was empathy. He understood the salesman's position, respected the dealer's need to make a profit, and never made the negotiation personal. He created space for everyone to maintain dignity while achieving his goal. This is empathy in action: seeing the full picture, understanding all stakeholders, and finding solutions that honor everyone's humanity while still achieving your objectives.

Grandfather Minks demonstrated a different but equally powerful form of negotiation, one that would prove even more revolutionary in shaping my understanding of how to advocate for others. His approach was rooted in something our culture desperately lacks: the courage to have uncomfortable conversations with genuine warmth.

Despite the discrimination he faced, Grandfather Minks developed an extraordinary ability to disarm even the most difficult people. But what made him truly dangerous as a negotiator was his complete comfort with topics that made everyone else squirm.

"Why wouldn't they like me?" he'd say with genuine curiosity when someone treated him poorly. "If they don't, that's their problem." This wasn't arrogance. It was empathy turned inward, a deep understanding that his worth wasn't determined by others' limitations or prejudices.

But here's what set him apart from every other kind person I've ever known: he talked about money the way most people discussed the weather.

In an era when discussing finances was considered vulgar, especially for women, Grandfather Minks treated money conversations as naturally as breathing. He didn't whisper about salaries or dance around the topic of what things cost. He asked direct questions: "What are they paying you for that work? Do you think that's fair? What would it take for you to feel good about that deal?"

I remember sitting in his living room as a young girl, listening to him counsel friends and family members through financial decisions. While everyone else tiptoed around dollar amounts, he dove straight in. "Let's talk numbers," he'd say. "What do you need to make this work for your family?"

This comfort with financial transparency wasn't just personal philosophy. It was strategic empathy at work. He understood that money conversations are where power gets redistributed, where fairness gets negotiated, and where people's futures get decided. By refusing to treat these discussions as taboo, he gave everyone permission to advocate for themselves openly.

He taught me that the people who struggle most in negotiations are the ones who were taught that talking about money is impolite, that asking for more is greedy, that good people should be grateful for whatever they're offered. These cultural messages, he understood, were tools of economic oppression disguised as good manners.

His courage, combined with genuine kindness, taught me that successful negotiation isn't about winning at someone else's expense. It's about treating people fairly, recognizing when someone is trying to take advantage, and having enough self-respect to ask for what you need while never giving up until you achieve it.

This approach was revolutionary for its time and remains rare today. Most people either avoid money conversations entirely or approach them with anxiety and discomfort. Grandfather Minks treated financial advocacy as an act of love, both for himself and for anyone he cared about.

Years later, when I began coaching executives through compensation negotiations, I realized I was channeling his spirit every time I helped someone get comfortable with saying, "That initial offer doesn't work for me. What other options do we have?" The tactical approach might come from Grandfather Merritt's playbook, but the courage to have these conversations at all? That came directly from watching Grandfather Minks treat every money discussion as an opportunity to ensure people got what they deserved.

Despite these powerful examples, there was one crucial area my grandfathers didn't prepare me for: negotiating my own compensation. Perhaps it was the era, or perhaps they assumed someone would teach me, but I entered my career completely unprepared for this essential skill. When I calculated the cumulative impact of accepting initial offers throughout my early career, the cost was staggering.

But this painful realization also illuminated something profound: empathy without action is incomplete. My grandfathers had given me the tools to understand people, to approach conflicts with respect and strategic thinking, and to persist with dignity. However, they hadn't explicitly connected these skills to self-advocacy in professional settings. The missing piece was the understanding that empathy must extend to yourself—and your own worth.

My early career as an executive recruiter was the laboratory where everything clicked into place. I witnessed firsthand how negotiation skills directly impacted people's ability to care for their families and secure their futures. Even $10,000 left on the table could have lifelong implications for financial security, children's education, and retirement planning.

This is when I realized that by applying everything I learned from my grandfathers to helping professionals negotiate their compensation, I could ensure they had greater opportunities and more choices. Money may not buy happiness, but it absolutely buys choices, and the right choices reduce stress while creating pathways to a more fulfilling life.

The challenge I noticed in my industry was pervasive: a widespread inability and lack of confidence around negotiating and advocating for oneself. This gap was particularly pronounced among women and other underrepresented groups who had been culturally conditioned to accept what was offered rather than ask for what they deserved.

This became my mission. I began developing frameworks that combined the strategic research approach I learned from Grandfather Merritt with the relationship-building and persistent kindness I observed in Grandfather Minks. The result was a negotiation methodology rooted in empathy but designed to achieve concrete results.

I've discovered that empathy is not just compatible with effective negotiation—it's the secret weapon that makes negotiation truly powerful. This revelation emerged from watching hundreds of executives transform their careers once they understood how to see negotiations through everyone's eyes.

Take Sarah, a brilliant CFO candidate who was terrified to negotiate her offer because she didn't want to seem "difficult." When we first spoke, she was ready to accept a salary that was $40,000 below market rate because the hiring manager had mentioned budget constraints. But instead of pushing her to demand more money, we started by exploring what was really happening on the other side of the table.

The hiring manager wasn't trying to lowball her. He was genuinely concerned about internal equity with existing executives and had been burned by previous negotiations that turned contentious. Once Sarah understood these dynamics, everything changed.

Rather than approaching the conversation as a battle over numbers, she reframed her negotiation around their mutual success. She acknowledged their equity concerns upfront and proposed a compensation structure that included performance bonuses tied to specific financial improvements the company needed.

Most importantly, she approached every conversation from genuine curiosity about making the arrangement work for everyone. The result wasn't just a compensation package that exceeded her original request. It was the beginning of a collaborative relationship that made her incredibly successful in the role because the hiring manager felt heard and respected throughout the process.

This is what empathy looks like in high-stakes negotiations. It's not about being accommodating. It's about understanding all the forces at play so you can craft solutions that work for everyone while still achieving your goals.

Today, my everyday habits and practices keep empathy at the center of my work by focusing on those who are often first to be disrespected, marginalized, or overlooked. I've learned that empathy is more about action than understanding. It's not enough to see different perspectives. Real empathy means working to create more equitable outcomes. This means actively seeking out opportunities to coach and mentor professionals who haven't had access to negotiation training. It means developing resources and frameworks that level the playing field for people who weren't taught these skills in their families or professional networks. It means speaking at conferences and industry events to share these strategies more broadly, reaching executives who might otherwise never learn to advocate effectively for themselves.

I lead workshops on "Negotiating Like Your Grandfather," where I teach the combination of thorough preparation, strategic thinking, relationship building, and persistent kindness that my grandfathers modeled. Participants learn that effective negotiation isn't about being aggressive or manipulative. It's about being prepared, respectful, empathetic, and unwilling to settle for less than they deserve.

The most rewarding aspect of this work is watching the ripple effects. When executives learn to negotiate empathetically and effectively, they don't just improve their own financial outcomes. They model these behaviors for their teams, creating organizational cultures where advocacy and fair compensation become normalized. They mentor other professionals, passing along skills that might otherwise take decades to develop.

I've seen clients who mastered these techniques go on to negotiate not just for themselves but for their entire departments, securing better compensation and working conditions for dozens of employees. I've watched women who were terrified to ask for a $5,000 raise become confident advocates who secure six-figure increases and then teach other women to do the same.

This multiplying effect is empathy's greatest power. When we learn to advocate for ourselves with skill and compassion, we create space for others to do the same. We challenge systems that undervalue people and create new norms that recognize everyone's worth.

The challenge in our industry remains significant. Too many talented professionals continue to leave money on the table because they were never taught that negotiation is both acceptable and essential. Too many organizations miss opportunities to retain and develop their best people because they don't understand how empathetic negotiation can strengthen rather than strain professional relationships.

But I'm optimistic about the future. Every executive who learns these skills becomes a teacher. Every successful negotiation creates a precedent for the next person.

Every conversation that begins with empathy and ends with mutual respect moves us closer to a professional world where everyone's worth is recognized and rewarded appropriately.

My grandfathers taught me that empathy isn't passive sympathy; it's active understanding that leads to purposeful action. The $2.8 million I lost taught me that empathy without action is incomplete. But empathy combined with strategic thinking, thorough preparation, and persistent advocacy? That's a force that can transform careers, organizations, and industries.

Today, when I sit across from executives who are terrified to ask for what they deserve, I see my twenty-three-year-old self. I also see the grandfathers who believed in me before I believed in myself. I see the possibility of conversations that begin with respect and end with mutual success. I see the ripple effects of empathetic advocacy spreading through organizations and industries, creating more equitable outcomes for everyone. That's the wild effect of kindness in action: it doesn't just change individual outcomes. It changes systems.

I miss my grandfathers deeply, but the lessons my grandfathers taught me about respect, preparation, and persistent kindness continue to drive positive change in boardrooms across the country. That's empathy's greatest power: it doesn't just transform moments. It transforms lives, careers, and the systems that shape how we value each other's contributions.

And sometimes, it can ensure the next generation never has to learn the $2.8 million lesson the hard way—a lesson worth more than any champagne-colored Cadillac.

MICHELLE MERRITT

Michelle Merritt is a recognized executive career expert, national speaker, and Chief Strategy Officer at D&S Executive Career Management. She has guided hundreds of C-suite leaders through career pivots and strategic visibility-building, combining her background in corporate HR, leadership development, and executive search with extensive board experience, serving on 30+ boards overseeing $1B+ in assets.

As a thought leader and keynote speaker, Michelle empowers senior executives to lead their careers as intentionally as they lead their organizations. She addresses audiences on executive leadership, career strategy, compensation negotiation, and breaking into the boardroom.

Currently serving as Vice President of the Westfield Police Department Merit Commission, Michelle is a recipient of the Civilian Award for Excellence from the 122nd Fighter Wing of the Air National Guard. An avid reader and Guinness World Record holder, she enjoys entertaining and hosting memorable gatherings in her Indianapolis home.

www.dscareermanagement.com
www.linkedin.com/in/michellemerritt

4

FOURTEEN HEARTS

BY SHAY MICHELLE DRAPEAU

Fourteen kids saved my life.

A dried-out turkey carcass sat in the center of the impromptu buffet table. I could hear Toni's warning. My first born, knowing her mother so well, predicted that bringing the buffet table out of garage purgatory was risking it gaining a semi-permanent address upstairs, far past Thanksgiving. The cheesy garlic Hawaiian rolls Shana made were the first to go, yet their dish remained. Michael's macaroni and cheese was a big hit. No one touched the chicken nuggets and fries that had ventured from New Jersey. A warm smile formed as I remembered Victor and Jason teasing me for not being clear about the chicken I actually wanted them to bring. Everyone was grateful that Elliot purchased the Oreo pie instead of making it. Easton blessed us with his flan, and I coveted the first slice as *My Precious*. My jokes throughout the night grew increasingly ageist, so I was unceremoniously told to go play with friends my own age.

My smirk the next morning, as I began gathering dishes, was one of maternal pride. The remnants of the night told a beautiful story: after dinner, there had been an attempt to clean. A few dishes made it into the sink, but the Jersey chicken and fries were still in the oven. I added the turkey carcass to a pot to make broth. The Oreo pie plate was at the top of the garbage heap, someone having used a finger to scrape the last bite. The hangout spot, formerly my garage, was riddled with character sheets, mini figures of dragons and orcs, and cups with the remains of soda. They'd played Dungeons & Dragons into the early hours of the morning yet again.

The video game controllers were on the couch. The giant Yogibo pillow sat in the middle of the floor. My youngest child, Ash and their bestie, had finally lured their elders-in-age-only into a PS5 battle. The birthday cake my cousin brought wasn't completely devoured, but two of my sweet potato pies were gone. No pans in sight. Shana cried the first time she tasted my grandmother's recipe, so now she gets her own each year. I would later find the second pie in my daughter's room with several forkfuls missing.

Having invited my kids' friends for a Friendsgiving, I felt like the proud mom who lived in a shoe. I'd borrowed these kids with the blessing of their parents. I'd borrowed them a lot over the previous year. Holding space was passing through the garage, laughing too hard at their cringe-worthy jokes, collecting cash they'd added to the Pizza Jar, or sitting on my couch, talking a teen through the latest social drama. They gave me purpose when I was empty.

Vincent, my baby from New Jersey.

Teddy and Green, my daughter's partners, who quickly became part of the family.

Dove, "Little Brother" to my daughter.

Shana, the first to call me Mom and steal my shampoo.

Michael, my gentle giant and Beyhive bestie, who has all the tea.

Easton, who rarely accepts hugs but will ask for advice.

Eliot, the one I've teased since kindergarten.

Ryan, the quiet, funny one with a love for bread and animals—and has great hair.

Riri and Austin, the couple who commute for Dungeons & Dragons.

Aiden, Ash's best friend, who spends as much time at my house as the teens.

My life had become gray and dreary during my favorite season of the year. But, as seasons change, I had to *choose* to do the same. All these kids in my home pulled out of me something I thought I'd lost. In a season of gratitude, I found myself open to caring, loving, and holding space. But before I could truly face where I was going, I had to forgive myself for giving up my voice and safety for far too long.

For too many years, loving my husband had become my sole responsibility. I thought that by supporting him through his burnout, surgeries, and childhood trauma, I was being a good and dutiful wife. The day I found my youngest hiding from our latest argument was when I realized I'd sacrificed their calm home for my role as emotional support woman. As an empath, I am proud of my ability to sense the emotional needs of others. However, allowing my partner's emotions to trump those of my children crumbled everything I knew about being a mother.

After two years of therapy—solo, family, and couples—I was diagnosed with empathy fatigue. I apparently no longer had the capacity to be someone's confidant, support, or person. I'd poured so much into my partner, friends, and family that I had bottomed out. Emotional burnout comes with depression, fatigue, fear that you'll never feel again, fear that you've let people down, anxiety over not being enough, and the sinking feeling of not being able to summon one iota of care when someone is breaking right in front of you.

I used to joke, "My husband has a PhD in me." He knew my moods and modes. He also knew how to use them. He once admitted to deliberately saying things wrong, knowing I'd obsess over the details. If I corrected him, I was "always correcting" him. When I stayed silent, he'd tell me I was judgmental anyway. For over a year, I trusted his memory over my own, even seeing doctors for memory lapses I didn't actually have.

The truth finally came out one night: "You've never been critical or judgmental. I told you that you were like your mother because I knew it would hurt you." I cried until my emotional cup was dry, cracked, and splintered.

Three months later, a behavior I'd yet to recognize became the catalyst to wake me up. He'd shut me down, yet again. My voice was silenced as I tried to help with the latest work or social upheavals. My advice was met with vitriol. "You don't understand this, so you can't comment. You have no idea what you're talking about."

The next morning, he approached me to tell me he'd had an idea. As he regurgitated my exact words with flourish— as if the muse sat in his lap and whispered them to him— my mind cleared. Images of past conversations played out like a movie. I lay in bed for hours, reliving all the times I'd donated to his *epiphanies*. I recounted the number of times he would tell everyone I was brilliant, but shut down my projects in private. With the dusting off of each memory, my body sank deeper into the softness of my mattress.

That moment of drowning was a breaking point. The end was inevitable.

The night he walked out, I felt the final drop of empathy leave my body. For years, I sat in a fog, weightless, chilled, unable to find my feet. The man who had once been my husband looked at me with disgust. No. Not my husband. The man I loved was already gone. This one leaving was giving my family the reprieve we needed. I'd felt it in that moment. The fog was lifting. Without it, my surroundings began to take shape. There were no walls, no misconceptions. No more. I would have emotional safety. I demanded it.

I stayed because I watched my mother, grandmother, and aunts struggle as single mothers. I stayed so my kids would know their father. I stayed because I loved him. My love wasn't strong enough to keep my sense of self safe. The emotional safety I provided wasn't enough. The emotional safety I sought from my partner was gone.

In the years that led up to the eventual dissolution of our marriage, my kids watched. Fourteen pairs of eyes watched as I became a smaller version of myself in my own home. They saw me accept a fate that I didn't deserve. They watched as my husband morphed from dutiful father to broken kid.

He left in the night. No goodbye. No text. Just gone. It wasn't supposed to be forever, just space for the time being. This felt like the other shoe had finally dropped. I felt empty without him, but I knew I'd find myself in the space he left behind.

My daughter Toni was closing out her junior year, and the coming summer would be her last as a child. I was focused on spending time with my two favorite people, my babies. Toni and Ash grew into their independence, but I wanted them to stay close. I established an open-door policy. Any friend I approved of had carte blanche entry to our home.

Not knowing how to cope with my new status as a single mom, I became a walking "yes" machine, giving my kids as much as my limited budget would allow. But during a family trip to see my bestie, I saw what they really needed. Antiquing with my best friend, their Auntie Amy, and feeding her pet bunny with her husband, Uncle Gabe, mattered more than trauma-triggering chats, an overly eventful calendar, and trips to the mall. What they wanted and needed most was time and attention. What I thought would be a boring weekend turned into a reprieve from the transition-in-process they had to return to. They didn't need me to keep busy.

They needed me to provide stability and safety. They needed their mother back.

The Dungeons & Dragons group had already established a stronghold in my garage, so I allowed my twelve-year-old to have video game night at the same time in the living room. It was a weekly tradition I was glad to reestablish. With a house full of teens and preteens, I was inundated with hormones, drama, crude jokes, mood swings, and an abundance of laughter. I loved every minute of it.

Toni crafted a gaming setup out of our dining room table, a table she crafted by hand, and a discarded table from trash day. She stood in the center of the room as Dungeon Master of the improvised melee, which included card decks, binders, and more dice than a casino in a rainbow of colors and materials. The others hung on her every word, responding as ten-foot ogres, druids, and rogues. I was proud of her improvised storytelling. I laughed at the reactions, sympathized with the deaths, and cheered at the triumphs.

Each week, I looked forward to hosting this makeshift family. I fed them. We joked, ate, and cried together. I talked them through some tough issues, talks that may seem small to them, but made a world of difference to me. Given the opportunity to care without reciprocation, to not be wary of why someone needed me, allowed me to trust my emotions again. It allowed me to see myself in each of them. Their vulnerability, loyalty to each other, and social resilience reminded me that I didn't have to go through this transition alone.

Their weekly games went from nights of me constantly making sure they were okay to them coaxing me out of the house. They'd watched as I tried to find myself again. They'd seen the solo dates and new hobbies. When I was down on myself, worried how I'd go on, one of them would call me Mom, and I'd feel ten feet tall. One night, as my kids encouraged me to go out for a bit (it didn't take much pushing), I asked the group of teens and tweens if anyone needed a hug before I left. A small chorus of "Me!" and "I'll take one!" followed. My heart was full as I took four different young souls into my arms.

Friendsgiving 2024 was one of the proudest meals I've hosted in seventeen years. The day after Thanksgiving, with half a turkey, a full pan of my grandmother's dressing (as requested), and a few desserts left, fourteen kids came together to give thanks. Each dish to supplement the meal was created (or purchased) with love, and no one ate until all but one had arrived. I was proud of our buffet spread of macaroni and cheese, garlic Hawaiian rolls, chicken and fries, ribs, greens, cornbread, Oreo pie, homemade flan, and other favorites. I watched as friends from the neighborhood, online games, and school came together to claim each other as family. They saved me from falling back into depression and spending days in my marshmallow bed. It inspired me to reconnect with my own friend groups.

I found the path to empathy with my teens, but I reclaimed that empathy in the women I surrounded myself with.

Two days after my husband left, I was sitting in the car he'd convinced me to lease when an old friend wandered by. She was on a walk, and I invited her into the car. Bridget, like so many of the women I'd newly befriended, was also going through a divorce. We went for a drink. I unloaded my story, receiving the same response I had for the last six months. Shock and disbelief that the man they knew as my husband could do all he'd done to break me. But, once over the shock, Bridget related. No, divorce and single motherhood weren't going to be easy. There was doubt, fear, anxiety, and days of depression. I would miss him, the life we had, and the future we had planned. We would both have to learn who we were without one another. I would have to choose: accept what is, to let go of what was, or return to what was and let go of the freedom that could be.

Nights with Bridget and fellow divorcées become more frequent. Nights of long chats where I learned that I wasn't alone in how I felt. Each validation was a building block clicking into place. Slowly, as each woman shared more of themselves, the picture of who I was began to fade. In its place was a path forward. It wasn't the first amazing group of women I found to hold me up when my self-confidence began to break, and it wouldn't be the last.

I met Helena when she joined a workshop I co-led for our local library. Her empathy stood out, especially in a group about diversity, equity, and inclusion. So when she welcomed me into her home, I knew I could simply be myself.

"Come over for a drink," she said over the phone.

I looked down at my PJs and slippers. I needed a friend, so I put on my bra and got in the car. I didn't expect to walk into her home and find a speakeasy with a full bar, library, bathroom, and a stage.

"Helena, this is amazing! May I?" I held out my phone.

"Go ahead," she smiled.

I recorded, taking it all in. I was in awe of the sanctuary she'd built for her family.

We settled into spinning fabric chairs with glasses of wine. My awe gave way to my jaw, and my mouth sat agape.

"Wanna sing?"

I must have looked like the teary-eyed emoji. A stage? A speakeasy? Of course I wanted to!

"Considering I put my bra on for you, yes!"

"You never have to put a bra on for me. This is a bra-optional basement."

That night with Helena was the first snowflake that, over time, snowballed into connections with more amazing women from town. I'd lived there fifteen years without finding a group that felt like home. Then, Bra-Optional Basement Karaoke (BOBK) was born. There were three rules: 1. Everybody sings. 2. Unconditional support. (No judgment.) 3. Bra-optional means come as you are.

Not everyone in BOBK knew me beforehand, but they got to know a version of me that I'd kept hidden. In that space, I didn't have to defend my lack of a "real" job or my imperfect marriage. I could sing musical theater, pop, or raunchy rap (thanks to our friend, Mina) without apology.

Karaoke nights expanded into brunches, a wedding, movies under the stars, babysitting swaps, and enough laughter to fill a genie bottle. When I revealed my lowest point—my failing marriage—they were surprised, but didn't flinch. They sat with me in my anger, my fear, and my elation. They celebrated my freedom just like we celebrated nuptials, new jobs, and nannies. I feared being a pariah, but I was seen, heard, and lifted up in music.

I found strength in these women. Nights in front of the mic or swapping divorce tales healed me more than therapy. They showed me I wasn't broken. I was transforming. And they would be there no matter how far I fell to pick me up.

I chose to accept life as a single mom. Helena and Bridget were the catalysts for a new version of myself. I focused on getting my kids through the transition. When I asked my youngest how they were coping with our new normal, they answered:

"I don't know. But it's calmer now. And you're happier now."

I leaned into the calm. I found a new job working in member services at the YMCA. I took the position to close the gap between what I wasn't making in my business and what I needed to pay the rent. It was fun to be around a diverse collection of people again, the perfect job to show me that I could relate to people without having to give all of myself to be seen. I gave my children stability. Waking up at 4:30 a.m. each morning, I found a sustainable rhythm that gave my kids predictability. Our command center included all the activities we had for the month. Monday was grocery day. My daughter became an even better big sister, encouraging and supportive.

Bit by bit, I rebuilt my love for people and socializing. I no longer felt drained listening to people rant. I didn't have to. I learned to set boundaries. When I am at capacity for negativity, I say so. Friends understand when I tell them, "I don't have space for this right now. Could we talk in an hour when I might be more receptive?" There is a usual response that culminates in, "Of course. Fix *your* crown first."

I'm grateful for the empathy-filled spaces I've carved out for myself. I have a collective of spaces where I am safe, seen, and emotionally held. I have spaces where I get as much as I give without a tally board. I have the support of women who know who I am and don't ever ask me to change.

Fourteen kids pulled me out of depression, showing me how to feel again. My sisters showed up for me, reminding me what it means to trust myself to have fun. I proved to myself that empathy given is empathy refreshed. I have multiple pools to draw from to fill my cup to overflowing. My cup overflows so I can give from the saucer.

Names were changed to protect the young and the young at heart.

SHAY MICHELLE DRAPEAU

Shay Michelle Drapeau is a best-selling author, certified personal development coach, and founder of She Breathes Life™, a movement and community dedicated to helping women and femmes reclaim their voice, worth, and wellness.

Known for her warm, bold approach, Shay creates safe, soul-nourishing spaces for healing, storytelling, and midlife resets—guiding those navigating transition, trauma, or transformation with empathy and power. She is one of the best-selling authors of *Got A Light*, a multi-author book sharing stories of moments that sparked personal change, and *Woo Woo,* where Shay shares her story of building faith and spirituality into her life.

Through her coaching programs, podcast, and live workshops, Shay supports women in rewriting the narratives they've outgrown and breathing life into the next chapter. Whether she's holding space for truth-telling, teaching women to set boundaries like a Queen, or helping creatives rediscover their spark, Shay shows up with heart, humor, and hope—reminding us all that healing is possible, purpose is personal, and you are always worth the rewrite.

www.linkedin.com/in/sharondrapeau
www.instagram.com/sharondrapeau
www.instagram.com/shebreatheslife
www.facebook.com/shebreatheslife
www.shebreatheslife.com

5

SOFT STRENGTH

BY SARAH SOUCIE EYBERG

"I can't do this! I cannot do one more thing today. I am not a machine!"

I screamed so loudly I could feel the blood in my throat, pounding both my fists over and over on the kitchen table. I was ten minutes late to my seventh phone conference in three hours. I got distracted chopping vegetables for chili in the crockpot for dinner and missed the start time for a new client consult.

Tears burned in the back of my eyes and began to pour down my cheeks as I shakily explained to my deer-in-the-headlights husband what my day had been like so far. We've been married a long time now, and he knows the burnout warning signs as well as I do. The biggest sign is always an outsized reaction to normal everyday stressors.

I was tired—so tired. I didn't want to listen to one more person's sad story about how their illness or injury has kept them out of work. I didn't want to hear any more tales of financial distress and mounting medical bills, knowing the only solutions I can offer will take months or possibly years, and the odds are still against us. But that's the job.

I became a lawyer to help people—especially people who have a hard time helping themselves. So opening a Social Security Disability (SSDI) practice was a natural fit. Most firms that practice SSDI work are "high-volume" practices, meaning they have thousands of clients, and usually a near-constant turnover in staff. At these firms, clients are treated like file numbers, not people: calling in to find their case manager has changed yet again, and there's been no progress on the claim. Meeting their attorney for the first time hours before the hearing that they've been agonizing over for the last eighteen months.

I learned firsthand about these client experiences in my role as a contract attorney through a large company whose business model was based on helping these high-volume national firms find in-person coverage for their thousands of hearings. The company essentially acted as a broker between these massive law firms and independent contract attorneys.

There were some personal bonuses to this type of work. It was very flexible, and I only took on hearings that fit in my schedule and were in geographic regions where I was willing to travel. When my children were very young, my partner and I were able to avoid the astronomical costs of traditional childcare and depend on family or the occasional babysitter on days I was attending hearings. I also didn't have to carry the administrative load of following clients' cases from application through multiple denials to the hearing itself. I got paid a flat fee for reviewing the file, preparing the claimant's testimony via telephone, attending the hearing, and a small amount of post-hearing paperwork.

However, there were also significant drawbacks to this model. I had no control over how the claim was prepared for the hearing and what evidence was gathered and submitted by the firm. In numerous cases, significant evidence was still outstanding or never requested when the hearing date arrived. Some claims were so poorly developed that the hearing actually couldn't go forward —a huge disservice to the claimant and a major annoyance to the administrative law judge and their staff.

Worse still was that the claimants I met with to prepare for the hearing often felt lost and confused about the process itself. They had spent months leaving messages or sending emails to firm staff that were ignored or lost and never returned. Often, I was the first person from

the firm they had actually spoken with. They were
frustrated and scared. This is the most important thing
going on in their lives—the stakes are incredibly high,
and this is their one shot to get these benefits.

I became very good at establishing credibility and trust
with these clients in a short period of time. Often, they
thanked me for being the most positive interaction they
had throughout their claim. Sometimes that pressure
became too much to bear. I couldn't have an "off day"
where I was less empathetic, compassionate, or
understanding. I couldn't just go through the motions
and wall myself off from the emotionality of the hearing
process—even if that's what I needed for myself that day.

My father, an accomplished trial attorney, made his
name by taking care of his clients. He made it his
mission to ensure all his clients felt cared for and
important. My father was a personal injury attorney,
meaning he represented people and their loved ones
who were catastrophically injured—and sometimes
killed—in motor vehicle crashes, gas explosions,
electrocutions, and other violent or harmful events.

I watched him give his heart over to these clients and
their families. He endeavored to learn everything he
could about them and really put himself in his clients'
shoes—sometimes literally. My father always prepared
for these cases by learning all he could about his clients.
He visited them in hospital rooms after their injuries. He

visited people in their homes or places of work. He asked questions not only related to the facts of the claim, but also to get to know who his clients were as people.

In one electrocution case he handled, he represented the wife and family of a construction worker, Daniel, who was fatally electrocuted when a dump truck driver raised the dump bed directly into overhead power lines.

The truck driver was blaming Daniel for his own death, accusing the deceased of directing the driver into the power lines. The driver said Daniel directed him to park under the power lines, and then, when the dump bed was raised and made contact with those power lines, Daniel approached the truck and grabbed onto the grab bar outside the driver's side door, electrocuting himself to death. Because the truck driver lived and Daniel died, the truck driver's testimony was the only eyewitness testimony available, and this testimony was very challenging to overcome.

Speaking with Daniel's coworkers and family, my father heard that Daniel was terrified of electricity and was extremely careful, to the point of being paranoid, on job sites. This clued my father into the unlikelihood that Daniel would be so careless as to direct the driver to park under the power lines. But again, Daniel was not there to tell his side of the story.

My father went to Daniel's home to speak with his wife and children. He sat at the kitchen table, where Daniel would drink his daily cup of coffee in the very early hours of the morning with his wife before he left for work. My father sat in Daniel's favorite chair in the living room. He even went so far as to lie on Daniel's side of the bed. My father took putting himself in his client's shoes as literally as anyone I've ever seen. He also put himself in Daniel's wife's shoes, as she recounted the police coming to her door to inform her of her husband's death. He pictured himself in her place, informing her children their father would not be coming home.

My father knew he needed all this information to make this terrible loss real for the jury. He also needed to come up with a plausible story to counter the truck driver's narrative. Besides anecdotal evidence from coworkers and supervisors about how careful Daniel always was around electricity and power lines, my father carefully reviewed the forensic evidence available. Daniel only had three burns on his body, as documented by the medical examiner. He had a very small burn on the thumb of his right hand and burns on the soles of each of his feet.

Through testimony from experts, my father was able to establish that the burn on Daniel's thumb was the most likely entrance wound from the electricity, and the burns on his feet were where the electricity exited his body. If Daniel's client had grasped the grab bar, as claimed by the dump truck driver, the entry wound most likely would have been on the palm of his left hand, as he was facing the driver on the driver's side of the truck when the accident occurred. Instead, the evidence supported that Daniel was likely waving his arms back and forth horizontally at chest level, a universal sign of "stop" or "no," and accidentally came in contact with the electrified dump truck, killing him almost instantly. The dump truck driver's story fell apart, bit by bit.

I can still see my father taking a marker and drawing on his own thumb the small burn mark found on Daniel's thumb to illustrate for the jury the most likely scenario. He also recounted the very last morning Daniel and his wife spent together for the jury in his opening statement. From when they woke up to her last words to him before he left for work on that fateful day, my father recounted for the jury step-by-step, putting the jury in Daniel's shoes, just like he had put himself.

This tragic death occurred when I was ten years old, and I still remember listening to my father practicing his opening statement like it was yesterday. In fact, he often asked my younger sister and me to listen to his openings and arguments to make sure they made sense when he spoke later to the jury. He took our honest feedback and improved on his themes and transitions to make sure he could provide the most straightforward and compelling story for the jury on behalf of his clients.

A by-product of this exercise was that I learned at a young age what it took to put myself in the shoes of another. To not only understand their pain or loss or fear, but to feel it myself—and then to articulate those feelings to others. It had a humongous impact on my life and my career trajectory. I wanted to help people like that too.

I was predisposed to empathy and compassion by nature. As a "sensitive kid," this showed up in many ways throughout my childhood. I was forever getting my feelings hurt, whether by rejection from my peers or teasing from my siblings. I cared very much about always doing well, and any criticism or constructive feedback often wounded me deeply. I have "big feelings," and I "take things personally." I have often been told I "can't take a joke" because I get upset when I am the subject of teasing. I rarely make jokes at someone else's expense, because I can't stand the thought of hurting their feelings either.

When I was around ten years old, I started taekwondo. I was always a bit of a tomboy, so a combat sport fit my personality much better than dance or gymnastics had. I really enjoyed martial arts and progressed quickly. I wasn't a stand-out star in competition, to be sure, but I was diligent and I learned fast, and I cared (of course) about doing well.

The classes had an impact on me outside the dojo as well. When I was in fifth grade, my parents attended parent-teacher conferences with my teacher, Mr. Dickens. I was an excellent student (fear of failure was a huge driver of this), so my conferences consisted mostly of my parents hearing how well I behaved and how diligent I was in my work. On this particular night, though, Mr. Dickens kept mentioning the "unusual crowd" I ran with at recess. After about the third mention of this, my father finally asked, "What do you mean by that?" Apparently, Mr. Dickens was surprised that, with my academic excellence and perfect behavior, I ran with "some of the toughest boys" in fifth grade. It was one of my father's favorite stories to tell about me.

Prior to my foray into martial arts, I would try to befriend these kids and play whatever rough-and-tumble game they were playing at recess. But because of my sensitivity, I would often come home in tears, having had my delicate feelings hurt. Post-taekwondo, that stopped happening. I was no longer picked on because I wasn't afraid to stand up for myself, talk shit back, or take someone down as necessitated by the situation. I still cried, and my feelings were still hurt, but I covered for it better and kept my breakdowns to myself. I couldn't turn the empathy off, even when it caused me pain.

My big heart continued to show up in all kinds of ways growing up. I was terrified of death and dying. I remember vividly when my grandmother got sick with cancer. My mother, siblings, and I were taking Grandma Helen out to eat. I was probably seven or eight at the time. My mom had asked me to go help Grandma through the parking lot. For whatever reason, that day, I didn't want to leave my mom's side, and rather than be an obedient child and help, I refused. Unfortunately, Grandma tripped on the curb and fell. I still remember her wig falling off and rolling across the parking lot in a gust of wind. When she went in to have her knee checked out post-fall, they discovered she had lung cancer.

Shortly after, I began to have recurring nightmares. They became so disruptive that I was afraid to go to sleep at night. My mother would lie down with me every night until I fell asleep. I remember wrapping my hands around the belt of her robe, desperately thinking that if she got up after I fell asleep, I would wake up. After my nightmares, I would go sleep on the floor in my parents' bedroom to feel safe. Eventually, the nightmares were so concerning that my parents took me to a child therapist —serious business in the '90s! The therapist eventually extracted the root of my disturbance: I thought I was the reason my grandma got cancer. In my young mind, I equated the fall in the parking lot with Grandma's cancer, and blamed myself for her getting sick.

But my sensitive nature was not all bad. I was sensitive to the needs of my friends and found it easy to relate to their problems and talk them through their own feelings.

I developed deep emotional intelligence and a strong moral compass. My sensitivity to right and wrong matured into a core value of integrity and a fierce sense of fairness, which set me on a path to becoming an advocate for others.

As I entered law school, my empathetic nature was again both a challenge and a benefit. Legal training requires its students to be objective, looking at the relevant material facts only and applying the rule of law. This can feel sterile, and sometimes the outcome feels "unfair" based on the story behind the case law. Law school also teaches you to argue a position, regardless of your personal feelings on the matter—much like debate class in high school or philosophy class in college. Logic, not feelings or passion, is considered the higher order.

But if you poll most first-year law students, they will tell you they are seeking a law degree because they want to help people and be of service. That was certainly my motivation. I saw the difference my dad made for people, not only in the results he got for his clients, but in how he made them feel cared for and a part of his family.

Law school is also a competitive environment. All the students are high-achieving, driven, and ambitious. Those previously existing tendencies are more heightened in the pressure cooker of legal education. Clerkships, fellowships, and job opportunities are often tied to GPA or class rank, with only the top tier of candidates even being interviewed for coveted positions. I was entering law school as a lifelong "A" student. I was quickly humbled by the amount of effort and dedication to achieve even a "B" average. The student with the top grade in each class was presented with a CALI Excellence for the Future award—named for the Center for Computer-Assisted Legal Instruction, a rare honor that many include on their resume.

In my second year of law school, I enrolled in the Reentry Clinic. In the clinic, we provided direct representation to individuals in a whole host of legal matters, including family law, expungement, and civil rights lawsuits. Our clients were individuals with criminal records suffering massive collateral consequences, including, but sadly not limited to, job loss, homelessness, and family separation. The Reentry Clinic helps those individuals fully reenter society by providing holistic representation to ensure recently released persons have the best opportunity to live a safe and fulfilling life.

My work in the Reentry Clinic was my first experience serving actual clients. Some of my cases felt more like social work than legal work, but they left a lasting impression. I helped one client secure housing and another put in job applications. I assisted another client who had been recently released from prison after conviction on identity theft-related charges. Most of her issues, though, stemmed from methamphetamine addiction. She was seeking to reestablish parenting time with her son, and I was able, through our advocacy at the clinic, to get her that precious time with her son. Eventually, she regained full custody after establishing herself in a new career and maintaining her sobriety. At the end of that semester, I was given a CALI Award for my work. It was completely unexpected—my proudest moment in law school.

My empathy—my ability to understand and feel my clients' feelings and help them feel heard—serves me well in my law practice. When I started my own law practice, my goal was to deliver client-centered services where my clients feel like more than a file number. At my firm, we optimize technology to enable us to serve more people without losing the personal touch. As my firm has grown, I have added staff who share my core values of humanizing and empowering our clients in an otherwise difficult and often unjust process.

In some parts of the country, SSDI cases can take two years on average to resolve. Roughly 60–70% of initial applications are denied. The process requires claimants to constantly prove how sick or impaired they are. Costly insurance plans still often have gaps, especially for the most chronically ill. Often this means constant co-pays, high deductibles, denied coverage for tests or specialists, expensive or uncovered treatment, and, in some cases, insurance lapses and medical bankruptcy. During this time, claimants often have no income, no access to healthcare, and growing debt, which can worsen their medical and mental health conditions. Many claimants lose their homes, savings, and/or retirement while waiting for decisions. This translates often into being "high need" clients in terms of communication and reassurance. The disability process is also full of roadblocks, denials, and disappointments, furthering the anxiety of my clients.

Sometimes, our clients die from their illnesses while they wait for their benefits. This is the saddest outcome of all —and far too common for my liking. My first client who died was a twenty-year-old woman with various illnesses, one of which was epilepsy. Her conditions were debilitating, but not life-threatening. I will never forget the day her mother called me to let me know she had passed. She had seized in her sleep and aspirated. Her mother found her. Worst of all was that we had filed for her benefits, but she was not able to sign the application before her death, so we weren't even able to get survivor's benefits for her mother.

I felt awful for her mother; as a mother myself, I can easily imagine the pain and trauma of coming upon your deceased child. I was devastated that I wasn't able to do more for her while she lived. Did I unnecessarily delay her case, or not give it my best effort, so she never got the claim started? This was not true, of course, but that didn't stop me from beating myself up about it. I had never grieved like this before. I knew her, but she wasn't a friend or family member. I felt the loss keenly, but there was no process for how to work through the grief.

Soon after, I hired an assistant. When she joined the firm, I found it much easier to explain the complex and heavy toll of client deaths to her, instead of holding it all by myself.

"It is an odd kind of grief that you may not have experienced before," I explained to her. "We know them, and we care about them. But they aren't our family or friends, and we won't experience their loss as much in our daily lives. But that doesn't mean it isn't grief, or it isn't important. It's okay to feel sad. It's normal for this to affect us and our work."

Acknowledging the grief and sitting in it is important to process properly. I always make sure my staff and I have the space and time to do this, because we have to take care of ourselves to keep going in this practice. But the work doesn't stop when we take that much-needed time, so then we get back to work.

Present day, pounding my fists on my kitchen table, tears threatening to roll down my face, I had reached a breaking point. My throat burned, and tension was a heavy weight on my chest. I could feel a headache forming just behind my eyes. This had been building, likely for weeks. I had seen the signs, but there was too much to do and too many places to be to slow down. I know I am extremely compassionate and empathetic. I will continue to take on cases, continue to raise my hand for volunteer opportunities because I like to be of service. I also know that without balance and proper boundaries, I will compassion myself into a coma.

I have put safeguards in place meant to protect and conserve my empathy. I am not shy about communicating to clients early that I don't answer emails and phone calls outside of business hours. I structure my schedule to limit the number of meetings or phone conferences in a day, a clearly imperfect system, but one we are constantly improving. I also will not work with jerks—not as staff, and not as clients. Still, even with these safeguards in place, sometimes I am overwhelmed or get burnt out. Sometimes, railing against the injustices of this "non-adversarial" disability process wears on me.

I make sure to get enough sleep. I don't drink alcohol. I exercise religiously. I coach my kids' sports teams. I get quality time with my husband. I laugh and cry and make time for social connections with my friends. This is a shield for my sensitive, empathetic heart. I take care to conserve my energy because I know my clients need it in a world where it feels to them like no one else is listening. I can be their advocate and champion, ensuring they feel heard and believed in a process designed to humiliate them. And that is my greatest strength.

So I picked up the phone and dialed the next potential client on my list. I apologized for being late. With tears still drying on my own cheeks, I asked, "Can you tell me a little about your health problems and why you are looking into Social Security Disability?" just as I have hundreds of times before.

Empathy is my strength. I bring it to every interaction. I know this can mean the world to someone else. So, for the next twenty minutes, I listen. I ask follow-up questions as they recount deeply personal experiences and their feelings of despair. And sometimes by the end of it, I can offer a solution, or at least a lifeboat.

SARAH SOUCIE EYBERG

Sarah Soucie Eyberg is the principal attorney of Soucie Eyberg Law, LLC, where she practices exclusively in Social Security Disability law. Known for her dedication and leadership, she serves in multiple legal organizations and was recently named a 2025 Rising Star Super Lawyer and Minnesota Lawyer's Attorney of the Year for Outstanding Service to the Profession. She now serves as Secretary of the Minnesota State Bar Association.

Outside her practice, Sarah is a published author, speaker, avid runner, softball coach, knitter, and deer hunter. She lives just outside the Twin Cities with her husband, Jason, their four children (Esme, Mina, Roland, and Walter), and a lively mix of pets and chickens.

Passionate about balance and community, Sarah brings the same energy and heart to her personal life as she does to her work—whether she's exploring the outdoors, fishing, knitting, or diving into her favorite fandoms.

Through it all, she stays grounded in what matters most: making a difference, supporting others, and leading with both passion and purpose.

www.facebook.com/mndisabilitylaw
www.linkedin.com/in/sarah-soucie-eyberg-1014a642
www.instagram.com/mndisabilitylawyer

6

HOLDING GRACE OR HOLDING GRUDGES

BY SANDY STEWART

*S*hoving a cheap push mower up a steep hill of long, wet grass was not my idea of a "hot girl summer."

I was a deer in headlights. When I first reported at 6 a.m. at the entrance to the county jail, along with some other fortunate souls, it was still dark, and I was anxious. It was my first day of the Sheriff's Weekend Alternative Program (SWAP). This was my lucky day, thanks to a compassionate judge who said at my sentencing, "I bet you've spent enough time in jail already." If I messed this up, I'd have to spend the rest of my sentence in jail. I'd take mowing lawns and sleeping in my own bed at night over more nights in a jail cell with a metal toilet, nasty water, and food I'm allergic to—except for the occasional apple. I'd had more of those nights than I care to recount.

There must have been seventy-five of us altogether that day, and the men outnumbered the women fifteen to one. I had my required gloves to protect my hands, and a collapsible cup to grab a swig of water when it was offered by the warden. It seemed to take forever to finish roll call and gather us in front of the massive storage building. By now, the sun was up and cooking, and we hadn't even started.

As soon as the storage building's big doors opened, those who had been there before ran to get the good equipment. The high-value items were first the blowers and edgers, and then the best lawn mowers. I ended up with a last-choice mower. Mowing a lawn wasn't completely foreign to me, but it had been decades. These were pull-start gas push mowers, which would have been fine if the lawns were flat, but this 130-acre property was nothing but steep hills.

We mowed in rows, about sixty of us side by side, in our bright hi-vis safety vests, while those lucky few with blowers and edgers came along behind us. We had to mow *up* those dang hills and *down* those dang hills. One woman told me, "This isn't my idea of a gym, but I think of it as a workout, and it goes by faster." Once I got the swing of it, I went full tilt on that lawn, and I was outpacing most of the guys who urged me to slow down. I was getting out some serious subconscious rage. The more grass my hungry mower and I chewed up, the better and stronger I felt. I was murdering that grass, and it felt so good, like a little release valve had switched on.

During those days of mowing lawns, cleaning prison buses, and scrubbing the officers' gym, I kept thinking: *How did I get here? This wasn't my upbringing. I feel so ashamed. How is this my life?*

Before jail, my life on paper seemed great. I had all the opportunities anyone else had, and I did pretty well with those. Before alcohol stopped being my friend, I owned a big company and had a lot of stressors. Some of my stress was appropriate stuff: making payroll, keeping clients happy, training new employees in any one of my nine locations. But there was some not-so-normal stuff too: unhealed trauma from sexual assaults, the exhaustion from keeping embarrassing things shoved under the rug, and a husband who couldn't–or wouldn't—support my desire to create a family.

And then there was me. Every time the shit hit the fan, I drank my feelings to cope. It was all so difficult, and I didn't know how to deal with it without falling apart. I was *so* afraid of falling apart.

All my life, I tried to be a "good girl." And to the outside world, I *was* a good girl. I learned from childhood about secrecy and self-reliance. I was taught by an older boy to "play" with him, but keep it a secret. I didn't think I could talk about the things that I had big feelings about, especially when his idea of "play" got more serious as I became a young teenager. I didn't tell anyone when it was happening.

I also didn't tell when in kindergarten, eight schoolmate boys threw me to the ground, lifted my little dress, and kissed me all over like an attack of bees. I thought, *Thank God Mom's asleep in the car and didn't see that.* I knew things like this were the way of the world, and I also knew not to tell, so I wouldn't get in trouble. I did not want her to be disappointed in me. I just crawled into the car and acted like nothing happened. But I was hollow inside.

I didn't tell when I was arrested in college for Public Intoxication, Minor in Possession, and giving False Information to the Police. I once told my college roommates that my new boyfriend date-raped me, but one of them said it wasn't true, and she didn't believe me.

I didn't tell anyone when I was roofied and raped in college. Without enough memories of the night, how would anyone believe me? What would I be subjected to, and would it even matter? Just another bag of dark and twisted memories to shove under the rug.

Yet there was one thing I'd always known for sure—I deeply wanted to be a mother. So, at thirty-seven, I married for the second time, believing this man would share and support that dream. I had made it very clear: "Don't even date me unless you're willing to have a baby with me and live in Austin." Well, we did get to Austin.

Seven years into our marriage, I brought up having a child (again). I was sure that once we decided, we'd make it work. Waiting for enough time or money could take forever—if we went for it, we'd figure it out. But unlike all the other times, he didn't reason his way out with a "not yet." This time was different. I'll never forget sitting in our new big, comfy swivel chairs in our century-old Austin bungalow when I brought it up. This time, he didn't give me any reason. This time, he put his foot down. "Sandy," he said. "This isn't going to happen. You are not going to have a child with me. If you want a child, you'll have to leave me."

What the hell? I thought to myself. *I mean, WHAT THE HELL? You tell me this now that it's almost too late for me? And zero conversation about it? I can't turn back the clock. I'm getting close to being too old to have a baby already. What about me? What about how I feel?*

Mid-forties, my biological clock was ticking louder and starting to fade at the same time. There wasn't enough time to get out of this marriage, find someone else, and get pregnant. While adoption as a single woman was also an option, the maze to even get there seemed impossible to navigate. I wished for some sudden magic sorcery to make my husband into a different man.

The reality was setting in: motherhood wasn't going to happen for me, even though I would have given up everything for it. It wasn't just a *wish* to become a mother. My whole life, I *knew* I was going to be a mother. All of my childhood books, family heirlooms, and my whole heart that I was going to pass down to my baby—now meaningless.

When he said we wouldn't have a baby, my heart sank, and all hope vanished in an instant. I didn't just feel let down; I felt robbed. My vision for my future was nothing but a massive black hole. My life suddenly felt like it was nothing: no meaning, no purpose, rudderless. Guess what you care about when your future is a black hole of nothing? Not a damn thing. I was in such a dark place and didn't give one crap about anything. I wasn't attempting to kill myself, but I would not have stopped an oncoming car.

I was careless, because frankly, I *couldn't* care less. After weeks of a series of very expensive and stupid random accidents, the biggest one came in the form of a DWI arrest. Still, I flat-out didn't care.

Things only got worse in that relationship, so my second DWI arrest four and a half years later—and mowing jailhouse lawns—was no surprise. I didn't think I had a drinking problem, and no one around me might have said so either. After all, I drank with those people, and they probably thought I was pretty authentic and had my shit together. But this, I'm saying, is exactly my point: just because I appeared to have it all together on the outside, how would anyone have any idea what was going on for me on the inside? I overdrank to cope when shit got treacherous. I thought I had a *broken-drunk-decision-maker* problem and an *I-just-happened-to-get-caught* problem. For a minute, when I got that second DWI arrest, I was scared straight. I absolutely didn't want to stay in trouble with the law. It was embarrassing, scary, and expensive.

Through my thirties and forties, self-reliance and independence were my badges of honor. I had to keep a brave face after all, and it was exhausting managing hard stuff on my own. I didn't understand what "self-care" truly meant. For a while, I thought it meant getting things off my to-do list, because that felt less stressful, but when that wasn't working, having a drink became my self-care routine. I would say I needed a drink to calm my heart down from the nonstop palpitations of stress—stress from demanding work, a financial roller coaster, an unfulfilling marriage, a seemingly rudderless life.

There came a point, however, that I could no longer feel a calming buzz from alcohol. It didn't happen overnight —it crept up gradually. Mid-probation from that second DWI, I was at Austin City Limits Music Festival, and it was *so* hot outside. I thought *I could have just one beer*. I thought having one ice-cold beer would be doable, but that one beer led to many more, and a blackout.

Coming to that next morning, I realized for the first time that I buzz-chased with more and more drinks while still not feeling anything—no buzz at all—and yet was drunk enough to black out. Then, it hit me: *This is happening all the time now.* As my friends came in to tell me they were going out for brunch, I asked, "What happened last night?" They told me that I had missed the band we went to see entirely because I had stationed myself at the bar inside. And once they got me home, they had to strip me down and throw me into the shower to clean up my puke. Something clicked. *I can't feel the effects of alcohol anymore. Is this what it means to be "pickled?"* Zero control and stupidity run amok, all to try to numb out the wreckage I had created, and there was another reason to drink: to ignore the embarrassment.

I had to make a change. I couldn't risk another legal run-in or the chaos from alcohol-fueled mistakes. When I decided to stop, I faced intense shame about my problem with it. It forced me to learn to handle my feelings, my fears, my disappointments, all in new ways. I had to face those dark and twisted memories I kept shoved under the rug if I was going to go through this life without my coping drinks.

At forty-seven, my sobriety came alongside other changes: living on my own after divorce, a forced diet change due to a new, sudden food sensitivity, and running my business on my own again. It took a few years, but I had to learn how to slow down and truly listen.

Deep self-care, I learned, isn't just surface things like a nap or a pedicure. It is listening when I need to walk away from a conversation or a friendship, talking about my feelings with a friend, saying the hard thing that needs to be said to repair a relationship, or vomiting them into a journal for my own reflection. If I get wrapped around the axle over something during my day now, I don't drink over it. I don't ignore it. Instead, I examine it to really understand my part, even if my part is that I took something personally when it had nothing to do with me. The freedom from making it right with honesty and openness far outweighs the courage required to revisit an uncomfortable exchange.

The number one thing I've learned is that I'm not wrong for the way I feel. I'm not wrong for my needs, my yearnings, my doubts, or my fears. I am allowed to take breaks and not overdo anything. I'm allowed to do whatever the hell my body, mind, and spirit need. And if I'm not staying connected to myself to really listen, I'll never know what that is. Once that lightbulb came on, I knew empathy for myself for the first time.

The gift of knowing compassion for myself comes with a bonus: compassion for others, and an understanding that other people also aren't wrong for the way they feel.

This was my first true understanding of empathy—for myself and for others.

In 2021, my understanding of empathy would deepen and take on a new shape. That year, my mother passed away at 81 years old from COVID-19. I loved her dearly, and when she passed, an immediate and unexpected wave came over me. In that instant, I could see her in my mind's eye, the human in her, with all her own wishes, fears, hopes, and scars on her heart. It was instantly clear to me that her life was her own journey, and she was this beautiful being in all its imperfect humanness who did the very best she could with what she had. It was not a conscious thought as much as it was a feeling, a knowing that whooshed through me and deepened my relationship with her immediately. I appreciated her even more for the whole person she was.

When I could see my mom's humanness with some kind of magical grace, it opened the door for me to give myself that same grace and not punish myself for my past mistakes or allow people to treat me poorly. After all, I was doing the best I could with what I knew at the time. Taking a hard look at the things I had always shoved under the rug is hard work, but the payoff is a feeling of freedom and a lighter load to carry (and not drink over).

Just three months after my mom passed away, I developed an ongoing illness. It took a bedridden year of tests to get a diagnosis. When I was finally diagnosed with a pancreatic disease and several other supporting conditions that won't get better, my outlook on my future narrowed.

Dealing with a hidden health condition is hard. I appear to be fine, so people expect me to be as fully capable as everyone else. But I had learned from a young age that some bodies need extra care.

When I was eleven years old, my father received a lifelong diagnosis: 100% renal failure. While a kidney transplant was a hope for a split second, his heart condition made it too great a risk. He was to dialyze regularly for the rest of his life. I was devastated when the doctor said we should expect him to live for five more years. *Would he even live to see me graduate high school?*

Then, he sat us down one day. "This doesn't define me," he said. "This doesn't define us. As humans, we have to drink water, get sleep, eat food. And now this is just another thing to have to do, like brushing our teeth. It doesn't define us. We will continue on with our lives."

My father understood the impact that his diagnosis had on our lives, and he had the empathy to know that our family needed to hear those words. And yet his words ring even more clear to me now, many years later, as I navigate the daily uncertainty of my own health. His words have never left me. As I say those words to myself now, I feel a profound self-empathy for the hardships my health condition creates. Thank you, Daddy, what a gift, all these years later.

Even as I write this, life continues to *life* at me. As I sat down to write, a longtime family friend passed away suddenly. I went from writing this chapter to writing her obituary. Then, my partner's father's health began to fail, and we were there for him during his final days. When life keeps life-ing, my body takes a hit. I'm still sick, and it feels so disheartening. *How will I ever be able to be a thriving member of society again?*

When these thoughts creep in, I think of something one of my sober friends said about tolerance and radical acceptance. "The discomfort and the struggle are about how I'm handling it, not about the thing itself." Oooh, that hit. It reminds me that I'm either holding grace or holding grudges. Everyone in my life, even those I am afraid of, those I'm disappointed by, and especially those who make me mad, is dealing with all kinds of things I know nothing about. The boy who mistreated me and taught me to keep secrets—I mean, where did he learn that? It doesn't mean their actions were acceptable, but it does help me to see that their actions had nothing to do with me. I can have empathy for those who have wronged me, and still it doesn't erase their poor decisions, nor my hurt from them.

After all, how would anyone know just by looking at me what I'm dealing with? What's happened to me? What have I learned from it all? If other people can't know about my life, how can I judge anyone else's? Like the instant empathy I had for my mother when she passed, I try to see everyone as someone who is simply doing the best they can with what they've been given. It feels like taking the high road, but it's also the most loving way of being in this world. Love thy neighbor, for real.

All of my experiences—with the law, abusing alcohol, sexual abuse, the whoosh of empathy for my mom, my health diagnosis—have given me a deep understanding and empathy for anyone working through their wounds. And for those who aren't ready to work through them, coping with them instead. I have to choose to hold grace instead of holding grudges.

Whatever success I find now comes from living my values out loud. I used to believe that I couldn't and shouldn't talk about certain things that happened to me. I used to believe that I not only could handle everything on my own, but that I was supposed to. I thought that's what being strong and independent meant. That kind of thinking keeps me holding secrets, and since I'm only as sick as my secrets, I must be open, transparent, and willing to show all my cards.

Even when I have bad days now, I know that self-empathy will get me through. I take stock of my daily experiences now with honest reflection to look at my part in any situation, and that process gives me power to rebuild my life with healthier relationships—and know my own worth—every single day. I no longer define or punish myself for my mistakes or the hardships I endure. Instead, I define myself by how I handle hard situations in all areas of my life, including at work.

My superpower at work is training and consulting. But it can be hard to be in front of a boardroom or with a client and hold space for them when the hard parts of my own life are a big distraction. Rather than ignoring those parts of my life, self-empathy is the path that gives me permission to work through them. It allows me to clear away all the gunk so that I can get back to my forte. I'm now running my business with newfound strength, choosing a healthy relationship, and taking care of my body and my spirit. I'm still learning and stretching—at 56 years old, nine years sober, and with my newfound tools for living, it's actually possible now to reclaim my power, rebuild my life, and own my worth every single day.

I think back on that summer when I was mowing lawns at the county jail. On my second day, I saw new women. They were standing with their rusty lawn mowers, looking more than a little lost. One said, "What do I do with this thing?" She gave a dismissive laugh, too embarrassed to make a scene. They were just like I was on my first day. I noticed the guys standing in a crowd about 30 yards away watching and snickering, as if this was entertaining to them. Not one would show them what to do. Even though I had only one day of experience, I did just that. *Screw those dudes*, I thought as I walked over to the women. "Do y'all need help? I used these yesterday, and I've got tips." I told each of them how to start the mower, stop the mower, and clean it from the clogged-up wet grass, which they would have to do a couple of dozen times a day.

I taught a dozen young women that day who were scared to be there, lost souls wanting to run for the hills. I created a posse with those women—proof that when life feels impossible, connection and empathy are the ingredients to holding grace.

SANDY STEWART

Sandy Stewart is a two-time best-selling author, speaker, and founder of Think Big, a coaching and training firm that helps businesses grow through strategic methodologies and referral ecosystems. A recognized expert on sustainable business growth, she equips leaders with proven methods to accelerate success through intentional partnerships.

Sandy shares her expertise through the Referral Growth Academy and her signature Strategic Alliance Accelerator, guiding business owners to spark real results and scale with confidence. She also leads strategic planning sessions that help organizations set clear, actionable goals for the year ahead.

Beyond her business work, Sandy serves as Vice President and Secretary for Tapestry Dance and is the founder of the Austin chapter of the National Association of Women Business Owners (NAWBO). She believes independent businesses are the backbone of the economy and is passionate about helping owners grow, thrive, and build lasting legacies.

www.linkedin.com/in/sandy-stewart-9534a/
www.instagram.com/thinkbigprogram
www.youtube.com/@ReferralGrowthAcademy

7

SHE WAS REAL TO ME

BY DEBRA BLUE

Listen to the wind blow, watch the sun rise.
Run in the shadows, damn your love, damn your
*   lies.*

I could feel the bass pumping in my chest, the lights flashing, making me the slightest bit woozy. We were both dressed in bodysuits and flowing sheer kimonos, wearing long blonde wigs, dancing the night away as Fleetmac Wood pumped out remixed versions of Fleetwood Mac songs. I felt so comfortable and free. I looked over, and Vanessa was spinning in circles to the music. I did not know it yet, but my beautiful friend would soon be torn from my life in the most unexpected way.

I met Vanessa years before, when she dated my old roommate, Ethan. I remember him saying, "I really want you to meet her—but keep an open mind because she's getting a divorce, she's ten years younger than me, and she used to be an addict." I was terrified he was making a poor choice, but I decided to trust him and, as he said, keep an open mind. Vanessa and I clicked right away when we met at a popular local coffee shop. She was smart, funny, caring, beautiful, and seemed to have an old soul. We talked for a long time. "I lived in New Orleans for a little while, and I wrote some teen science fiction books," she said. "But I did have to go to rehab for an addiction."

She and I quickly formed our own friendship, spending hours discussing life's challenges, the world around us, and drinking too much coffee. I was getting divorced at the time, and she was who I confided in. My self-confidence was at its lowest, and in my mind, I was a failure. "I feel old, washed up, unattractive. I wasted my youth," I cried.

"You're not any of those things," Vanessa replied. " You're just hurt, and you will get through it. I'm here for you."

Ethan, Vanessa, and I started planning creative nights. We would dress up and take photos all over town, a practice we maintained for quite a while. My favorite photos of myself are from this time; they made me feel strong and beautiful again. One image was taken in a hotel room: with stark white walls, a huge king-sized bed with ivory sheets, two women, a blonde and a brunette, obviously nude, one reading a noir novel and one looking at a book of erotica—only we had on Groucho Marx and Salvador Dali mustaches. The three of us cracked up at the proofs from that night as we worked together to create ideas for future shoots.

One afternoon, getting ready to go out for dinner, we were finishing our hair and makeup, and we both reached for deep red lipstick. It started out with just a simple eyebrow lift in the mirror from Vanessa, the kind you make when flirting with someone across a crowded room. I retorted with a duck face, my best imitation of a social media influencer. It very quickly turned into us making the most hilariously distorted faces we could think up until we doubled over with laughter. I took a photo of our reflection, a classic Vanessa and Debra moment. She matched my weird, and I loved her for it.

Ethan and Vanessa's relationship moved at the speed of light. Before I knew it, she was pregnant, and they were getting married. When she gave birth the first time, I was there. The memory of that day is still so vivid. The three of us walked on paths around the birthing center, and Ethan pulled a flower off a vine, handing it to Vanessa.

"What's this?" she asked.

He responded, "It's a honeysuckle; you suck the liquid out of the flower stem."

"You're joking," she retorted. "I'm not falling for that." Then, a look of childlike amazement as she tasted it.

Vanessa had been in labor for over twenty-four hours and was being moved from the birthing center to the hospital. She was exhausted and needed time to rest. The hospital sent everyone home, except Ethan. I would be called back when things started to progress. Unable to relax while I waited, I baked chocolate cupcakes just to have something to do with my hands. A couple of dozen later, the phone rang. It was Ethan: "Time to head back to the hospital."

The intention was for me to be in the room, but the hospital had limitations, so I impatiently waited and paced outside, pressing my ear against the door every couple of minutes. When I met their baby, my heart melted. Driving home that night, I sobbed and yelled into the sky, "Please, please keep this family safe. I'll give up on having another relationship if they don't have to go through the pain I just did with my divorce."

I don't think the universe heard me.

This beautiful woman pulled me into her family, something I had not felt for a long time. When they got pregnant a second time, I was in the room and filmed the birth. "Oh my gosh, oh my gosh, here it comes, oh fuck, oh gross, I just got sprayed with fluid," was what Vanessa would hear when she watched the video later. I became the godmother to both children, and Vanessa gave me the nickname "Mama Dos." It meant the world to me.

"If something ever happens to us, will you take care of the kids?" she asked me. "I know you will raise them the way we want, with the same values Ethan and I have." I wouldn't have thought to say anything other than yes, but at the time, I did not know that this was possibly a premonition.

I was not around many of my friends when they were new mothers, but she made it look so natural. One day after work, I walked in with gummy candy in hand. Instead of just giving one to her toddler, she made a learning game out of it. I snapped a photo to forever capture the sweet moment: Vanessa bent down next to the big red chair with her caramel-colored pixie cut and a warm smile on her face, while she held out a red letter E to her child and had them repeat the color and letter.

She and the children had a schedule for everything: eating, napping, planned activities, and even sections in the house for art, music, and playtime. In between all of that, she would tell me, "I'm so busy. I just need some alone time. I feel like I'm constantly trying to keep the house clean, plan dinner every night, and take care of these two all day and evening." Vanessa impressed me, and I tried to help out whenever I could, but I could sense the huge toll everything was taking on her.

We took beginner rock climbing lessons at separate gyms. When we finally climbed together, Vanessa studied the wall, then pointed to one of the white routes intended for beginners. As she started her ascent, her small, agile frame moved from one grip to the other like she was dancing with the wall. She reached her right arm up and grabbed a jug, her right leg stretched over to a foothold, her bodyweight shifted off her left leg until she found a good place to toe the wall. After climbing, we sat down to catch up.

"When the kids start school, do you think you'll start writing again since you'll have more time for yourself?" I asked. "You were published when you were younger; I bet you could be again."

Vanessa shrugged her shoulders. "I'm not really sure; I haven't thought about it," she said.

"One of these days, I really want to read your books— you still need to give me the titles and your pen name," I reminded her.

Not long after that, Ethan texted me a photo of Vanessa: emaciated frame, hollowed face, modeling a leopard print jacket that belonged to her toddler. I was horrified.

She looked so sick. I wanted to ask my friend if she was okay and why she felt the need to shrink herself away from the world. Torn between concern and not wanting to hurt her feelings, I replied with, "I know she's been really focused on her weight and working really hard to eat better and exercise more."

I regularly reached out to spend time with her and the children, but it seemed to happen less and less. I wondered if I had said or done something to upset her or push her away. Missing her, I texted Vanessa a selfie from my bathroom with rollers in my hair, no makeup, a naked-lipped duck face. Almost instantly, she replied with her own selfie: a matching duck face with a black turban on her head, clearly standing on her front porch where she had gone out to smoke. I could smell the cigarettes in my mind.

"Do you want to go climbing with me today?" she messaged after what seemed like months of no contact.

I replied: "I would love to, but I have a lot of homework to do. Let me take a break in a couple of hours and head over—but I'll only have one free hour."

Upon arriving at her house, Vanessa said, "I need to go pick up a refill for my vape. I'll drive."

"Why don't you let me drive?" I said. "I know you have driving anxiety; I don't mind at all."

"What, don't you trust me to drive?" she snapped, a cold glare in her eyes.

Instead of going to a vape shop close to her house and the climbing gym, Vanessa had me go to one about twenty minutes away. "They have what I need; the other places don't carry it." Upset by the amount of time the errand had taken and her strangeness about me driving, I ended up watching her climb for about ten minutes before I went home, reeling with annoyance.

Around the same time, she came over one evening and worked on a puzzle with me. "I am going to head out now, I'm meeting some friends downtown," she said.

"Haven't you been out all day doing extra work for a video?" I inquired. "I figured you would be tired and want to go home to see the kids."

Vanessa's smile dropped, her eyes narrowed. "Are you fucking judging me? I don't need my friends telling me what I should do. Ethan can watch them; I have them all the time."

I was caught off guard. "I'm sorry, I'm not judging you at all," I said. "I just assumed. I'm sorry. I hope you have fun tonight."

Two months later, my watch vibrated. Seeing that it was a text from Ethan, I grabbed my phone. The text read: "I was giving the children a bath, and Vanessa was getting ready to go out. She seemed very short-tempered, so I offered to take the kids to our family's house a day early so she could have some space and time alone. She threatened us." A wave of panic washed over me. I continued reading. "I had to call the police so they could watch us leave safely. We have been here about six weeks; I'm sorry for not reaching out sooner."

The message left me anxious, and I felt horrible for not knowing already. I had spent so much time with them over the past eight years that it seemed absurd I had not been in contact for that long. They would stay with family for months as a nightmare began to unfold, and the truth of Vanessa's return to drug use came to light.

She stayed in their house alone for well over a year, becoming more and more paranoid as the substances she was using changed her brain chemistry. This beautiful woman, who had been the sunshine in the room, a daughter, a wife, a mother, and a friend, was in turmoil. Scrolling through her social media posts, I witnessed a startling change. Pages once filled with memories of growing children, holidays, and fun times turned sinister, naming people whom she perceived as "the evil ones." Devastatingly, that list included my name. For the first time, I was afraid of her. This was not the Vanessa I knew and loved. I could not predict her actions anymore.

A family member went to check on her and take her food. They reported back that the house was a complete mess. Trash was everywhere, and holes had been knocked in the walls. They said she was complaining that someone had set up surveillance cameras inside the house to spy on her, and she wanted their help to disassemble them.

One night, Ethan reached out to me. "I just got a call from the fire department. There was a fire at the house." He was informed that Vanessa wanted to "make art" and took a small handheld torch to the drywall in the main bedroom. "The room caught on fire. Luckily, no one was harmed, and the house didn't burn completely down, but it's going to need extensive repairs." Even with the fire destruction and the house being condemned, the only way Ethan could get her off the property was by having her served with divorce and eviction papers.

Eventually, I asked, "Do you mind if I go look for some of her things for her family?"

"No," he responded. "I moved anything salvageable to the apartment behind the house, but it's a mess from Vanessa crashing there for a while. Be careful, there's broken glass from the window she knocked out."

As I walked in, the smell of rotting food made me gag. Clothing and trash were piled everywhere, like an episode of *Hoarders*. Then I saw them, the items I had hoped for: her sketchbooks. Only two had survived. One was small and didn't have much in it. Inside the second were some of her practice portrait drawings, but as I flipped through the pages, to my horror, the images turned to scratchy drawings of eerie figures staring and reaching out of the pages, like specters coming to get her. Sadness overwhelmed me, then profuse compassion and empathy for the horrible situation my friend was in. Then, I spotted a diary. Picking it up, I paused and contemplated whether reading it was a violation of her privacy. I dropped it, grabbed the sketchbooks, and left.

Vanessa returned to the main house after it was remodeled and lived there for a week or two. I went inside once I knew she was gone again. I took in the scene: another broken window where she entered, once again trash scattered in the rooms she lived in, a clogged toilet due to the water being off, candles and matches strewn about because there was no power. The stench hit me, a combination of the backed-up toilet and leftover food on the floor that was growing mold. I did my best to clean it up so Ethan didn't have to do it all himself. All I could think to say to Ethan was, "I'm so sorry you are having to go through all of this. I hate seeing how she was living. It makes me really sad for all of you."

When I was told Vanessa had been arrested, I made the mistake of looking at her mug shot: a distorted smile, almost sinister, that reminded me of the Joker; eyes glazed over, sores all over her face, no resemblance to her former self. She would tell her family, "A chip has been implanted into my brain; someone is trying to control me."

Then, she vanished. This was the friend who had come into my life like a whirlwind, a confidante, the one who helped me through the tough times and built me back up —and I could not repay her the favor.

I learned that, legally, not a lot can be done when an adult goes through a mental health crisis and refuses help. It has to get to the point where they are a threat to themselves or someone else. A "threat to themselves" means a short seventy-two-hour hold in a hospital that they can just walk out of; a "threat to someone else" could mean time in jail if a law has been broken.

Ethan, her family, and I still got together for holidays to keep things as normal for the kids as we could. At one point, I asked about her books. "Do you have any of the books she wrote, so I can finally read them?"

I was met with blank stares. "What are you talking about? She's not a published writer. She also changed her name to Vanessa a few years ago, did you know that?" My heart sank. Did I even know her?

Vanessa had shown me the person she wanted to be, not the person she had been early in her life. Looking back, and reading more about mental health struggles, I began to understand. But what she may not have realized is that she was real to me. She was my friend. I loved her. I had to grieve the loss of her, and I had to forgive myself for not picking up on the severity of her struggles. I would have done anything to help her through it.

Ethan explained the situation to their young children well: "Mommy's brain has been lying to her." Such a simple explanation for something so heavy, hurtful, and destructive. She was living in a different reality than the rest of us, one where she was paranoid, possibly hallucinating, feeling like she was being watched and controlled, and assuming everyone she knew was against her.

People never really know who someone is, what their truth is, what they have been through—only the part that they are willing to share. Vanessa unknowingly taught me to be kinder to everyone, to try and understand their feelings and perspective, to not judge, and to keep an open heart.

Vanessa was unable to break the chain. She could not free herself from mental illness. And I refuse to break the chain of the memories I have with her. I still picture her, spinning in circles to the music until she stopped, wild-eyed, laughing from the dizziness and tearing off her wig. The song was still playing as we moved out to a picnic table on the bar patio. The outside air was cool and fresh. She pulled out a cigarette and flicked her lighter, illuminating her glowing face. We sat and talked, sharing our wildest dreams, while the music played on for hours.

> *And if you don't love me now,*
> *You will never love me again.*
> *I can still hear you saying,*
> *You would never break the chain.*

DEBRA BLUE

Born into a military family, Debra was on the move from day one and learned how thrilling it can be to go to new places and learn about different people. This was the catalyst for her pursuing a cultural anthropology degree. The experience also meant she was frequently the "new kid" and learned the importance of kindness and empathy early in life.

After a short stint in NYC, Debra began a career in the tech industry that has spanned 24+ years and has allowed her to delve into her travel addiction. She constantly pushes herself to learn and try new things. Her favorites among them include: completing a half Ironman in 2013, hiking in the Himalayas in 2016, obtaining an MBA in 2018, visiting Antarctica in 2020 (before the world shut down), and becoming a best-selling author in 2023.

www.instagram.com/woman.spread
www.linkedin.com/in/debrablue

8

SOCKS, TIES, AND BAD GUYS

BY DAYNE WHITEHURST

I love mornings like this. In before everyone else, hidden away, free to blare Broadway show tunes without judgment while I knock out my to-do list. The tasks are relentless, yet I relish the satisfaction each time I cross one off. At twenty-four, I'm thriving as the hiring and training coordinator for a massive entertainment venue.

Rent has me singing, "Take me baby, or leave me," as I review new applications, prep for today's seven interviews, and verify that trainers and managers completed last night's day-one tasks in their new-hire training guides.

Arcade Technician? Check!

Bartender? Check!

Food Runner? Check!

Server? ...of course not.

I search the usual server hangouts. Nothing. The joy of the morning slips away when I read who was supposed to oversee the training last night. Just my luck, he's the opener today.

I collide with his cologne the moment I enter the back-of-house. Over the clang of the cooks prepping for lunch, I bravely greet today's manager. "Good morning, Trey! I can't find the new server's training guide from last night. Do you know where it is?"

He's irritatingly immaculate: royal-blue spotted socks peeking beneath perfectly pressed slacks and a complementary tie. It is a playful combo I begrudgingly enjoy, clashing with the brusque man who wears it. Trey flips the page on his clipboard, head and eyes down, then dismisses me with, "No clue."

Swallowing back the sting of rejection from yet another unhelpful conversation with this supposed manager, I try again. "Oh... okay. Did she come in last night?"

Without a hint of eye contact, he flatly states, "Don't know."

A few days later, the new server's training guide turns up under a stack of musty drink trays at the bar. After sorting through the sticky, incomplete pages, I work up the courage to approach Trey again. Near the host stand, I spot his colorfully striped socks and perfectly paired tie. With a betraying higher pitch, the words tumble out. "Hi, Trey! When you have a moment, would you sign off on the manager sections for your new server's training guide?" I extend the crinkled packet in his direction.

He lifts his eyes from his notes, not taking the packet or making a sound. He just stares at me, all eyebrows, like my existence is beneath him and an inconvenience.

My stomach sinks, and heat runs up my neck, turning red as I shove down my insecurities and stammer, "It's... so... I can ensure she... received all her training and submit it to Corporate as a completed training guide? And... I'm not able to do that without your signatures confirming it was completed...?"

Instead of offering help, he scoffs while shaking his head. Snapping his papers into a tidy stack, he brushes past me, leaving the guide and his crop-dust of cologne. I'm left standing with flushed cheeks and assaulted nostrils.

Shaken, I slink away to Kristen's office, our Special Events Manager and everyone's favorite person to work with. Her contagious laughter drifts down the hall, and even in my defeated mood, I can't help but smile. I picture her laughing with her whole body and wonder, *what could possibly be that funny?* Her warm smile and welcoming energy seem too big for the four windowless walls as I enter. She's wrapping up a call and waves me toward a chair beside her.

As she returns her headset, she swivels toward me, her voice bright and comforting. "Good morning! How did your new hires do in your orientation class the other day? You were really excited for this group."

I notice her take in my blotchy chest and watery eyes. Concern replaces cheer. "Oh no, what's wrong?"

It all comes pouring out. "Trey is always like this. He is so rude. Is there any wonder his department has the largest turnover? The most staff vacancies? I'm just trying to do my job. And I'm really good at it! I just really need him to do his part. How can you even stand that guy?"

When I run out of steam, Kristen leans back in her chair, thoughtful. She doesn't validate my sentiments by jumping in with judgment about Trey, or commiserating about how awful he is. Instead, with an inquisitive lift of her eyebrows, she suggests, "You could ask him about his socks."

I nearly choke. She might as well recommend I lick his big toe. I splutter, "What? No way I'm sucking up to that arrogant, conceited jerk. That is not happening."

Kristen doesn't try to convince me. Her only response is her "frog face"—that knowing, tight-lipped smile that signals she's said her piece, and I'm free to proceed as I wish. Lacking the backup I was hoping for, I sulked back to take refuge in my showtunes-less office.

It took years for her hidden wisdom to fully land. I could usually point to an incident or difference in opinion as to why I didn't get along with someone, but with Trey, I never knew. What I did know was that I cared about being helpful and kind, yet my good intentions were not enough to earn his cooperation—or a measure of courtesy in return.

Looking back, I was capable of empathy, generously so, when I could see someone's struggle or pain. But as a kid, some adults who should have kept me safe instead left me raw. Verbal abuse and abandonment were part of my everyday life. I learned to read "mean" or "bad" as a danger to avoid, not as a struggle to understand. As they do, those early defenses followed me into adulthood. When someone treated me, or others, in a way I perceived as wrong—like Trey had—my instinct was to label them toxic and retreat.

Cruelty can wound a child faster than love can heal it.

Over time, the fierce love and devotion of my father, paired with my own resilience, would give me the strength to confront the harm and learn new behaviors. But at twenty-four, consideration for those who expressed themselves differently than me was not yet on my radar. If I had paused to imagine Trey's perspective, the picture might have looked different:

Oh please... not this morning, Trey groans to himself. *Maybe if I keep my head down, she'll get that I'm busy and keep walking. Gah. No such luck; here she goes again, droning on and on about some inconsequential paperwork. What is she even talking about? Doesn't she understand I have twenty tasks to complete before the doors open in thirty minutes? Two servers called out this morning, the other manager is late... again. We didn't get out of here until 2:00 a.m. last night. Did I even sleep? My girlfriend hates this schedule and is threatening to leave.* Trey's eyes burn from exhaustion, and his head is throbbing. *I just can't deal with this self-centered kid again today.*

I couldn't grasp it then, but later, I saw that Kristen wasn't implying I should stroke his ego. She was showing me that I only approached Trey when I needed something, rather than finding a way to connect with what mattered to him.

The effort he put into his matching cashmere socks and silk tie was clearly a source of pride. Maybe a way to add brightness to his life. Asking about them could have opened a door to a relationship. Maybe not a friendship, but it could have paved the way for communication. For him to be comfortable enough to say to this sensitive young do-gooder, "Look, this paperwork is a low priority this time of year. Right now, we're just trying to keep our heads above water. Is there another way?"

Back then, I simply saw a roadblock to my to-do list, not the human behind it. I walked away feeling disrespected and unsupported, convinced Trey was a terrible manager—and if I'm honest, a terrible person. What never occurred to me was that my own narrow lens was just as much the problem.

Today, I decipher those moments differently. What feels like defiance or dismissal on the surface is often stress, exhaustion, or fear in disguise.

Empathy doesn't excuse poor behavior, but it changes how we interpret it. While the sock lesson had reshaped the way I connected with people, it didn't fully transform me until years later, when I became a mom. Parenthood has a way of holding up a mirror, reflecting not just who we are, but who we are becoming. Many years later, it did just that one sunny, not-a-cloud-in-the-sky Texas afternoon.

My two-year-old son and I are driving home from daycare, belting out "The wipers on the bus go swish, swish, swish," as we soak up the sunshine.

The smell of fresh-cut grass drifts in on the breeze as we ease down the tree-lined street near the elementary school. A gray sedan abruptly appears in my rearview, startling me. She's too close, swerving left and right, trying to get around us. It's down to one lane as the other is blocked for construction. *What do you want me to do? I'm trapped.* She's frightening me, her car unpredictable, so near it feels inevitable she'll slam into us. The sight of my son's carefree smile clashes with the threat filling my mirror.

The road opens to two lanes, and she guns it. In a flash of metal, she blasts past us, barely braking for the red light, going sixty miles an hour. I imagine a ball bouncing into the street chased by an unsuspecting child, and my blood ignites with rage, prickling my skin. My pulse hammers loud against the music. "The horn on the bus goes beep, bee—" I mute the song and glare at her speeding taillights with an explosion of internal accusations: *How dare you put my baby in danger? You should be ashamed of yourself. What is wrong with you?*

Through clenched teeth, I growl, "You are such a bad guy!"

From the back seat, my toddler comes to her defense. "She not bad guy."

I correct myself, huffing, "Oh, you're right. She is a bad *girl*."

His small voice is insistent. "She not bad guy."

My anger is in charge, and I lecture, "Yes. She is. There are babies on this road! She is speeding, and she is not being safe."

His precious little voice cracks, tears well up as he yells at me with clenched fists against his car seat, "SHE NOT BAD GUY!"

I'm snapped out of my own tantrum as if doused with cold water. My anger collapses. I take a calming breath in... and out... My heart rate settles, cooling my skin. Softly, I ask my son, "You don't think she's a bad guy?"

Still whimpering, he persists through his sniffles, "Not."

The car is silent, the music gone, the laughter stolen. I glimpse at my sweet boy in the rearview, longing to meet his big brown eyes, but his face is turned deliberately away, a punishment sharper than words.

I turn left at the light and gently ponder, *I wonder what would make me drive like that by a school?*

I wrestle with it, thinking, *I'd never ever do that.* Then it hits me. "If you were sick or hurt, I would drive faster than a rocket ship to get to you." After another beat, it sinks in. "Do you think maybe her baby is sick?"

He wipes his nose with the back of his little hand as he confirms, "Baby sick."

I had grown from centering on my own point of view to becoming curious about the stories behind people's actions. But my toddler guided my awareness to another level. I hadn't realized just how judgmental I could still be. I was scared for the safety of children. And, I was wrong. Two things can be true. I'm still in awe that my young son handed me one of the most priceless truths of my life: how unkind it is to slap someone with a label.

When I share this scene, people sometimes push back: "But what if she deserves it?" This is exactly the shift. Empathy isn't excusing or deciding who is worthy. It's about admitting we don't have all the facts. Maybe she was rushing to something inconsequential, or maybe she was racing toward something life-altering. I don't know. And accepting that is where it begins.

In the quiet that followed on the ride home, I promised my son I wouldn't label anyone "bad guy" again. More precisely, I was committing to fully embrace the lessons of empathy that kept finding their way to me. Since then, when we play or watch cartoons, I replace "bad guy" with "villain" to describe someone who is opposing the hero or is causing mischief. Where "bad guy" attacks identity, "villain" is about their role or their behavior.

A short time after this "bad guy" encounter, my promise was put to the test when a helicopter thudded over our street and police swarmed our neighborhood. When my son asked what was happening, the old me was tempted to explain, "The police are after a bad guy." But his earlier lesson echoed in my mind. I locked the doors and explained, "Someone broke the law, and now he's scared. He's hiding because he doesn't want to get in trouble. The police are trying to help him and keep everyone safe."

Those realizations deepened my understanding of empathy far beyond parenting. And thankfully, they arrived just in time. Not long after the hovering helicopter, I found myself on the receiving end of someone else's outburst.

As the plane lands, bumping up and down on the runway, so does my stomach—not from turbulence, but from the weight of the meeting ahead—a team visit quite different from our usual. Not full of laughter, inspiration, and ideas, but focused on resolution. Beneath the nerves, a steadiness anchors me, knowing I'm prepared and capable of handling the hard. Seventeen years have passed since Trey... years that have carried me further into leadership roles and onto a new company. De-escalation comes easily now, as my own triggers rarely lead the conversation. I can now find the person in each confrontation, a hard-earned skill that has become essential in my role as national sales director.

On the drive from the airport to the office, I review my notes with the many complaints about Erin, one of our group event managers, made by her colleagues. *"She's aggressive." "She's cold, even cruel." "It's not only us, she treats the guests like this too: sharp and dismissive."* I've come to know her well enough to see this isn't how she used to be. *What's going on behind this behavior? What could cause her to be acting like this? Is she okay?*

As the driver pulls into the lot, I close my notes and draw a steadying breath before heading inside. After a few cheerful hallway hellos, I knock softly and step into

Erin's office. It's devoid of color and washed in fluorescent lights, the buzzing bulbs the only sound. Tension radiates off her, pressing against me. Her smile doesn't match her eyes, and her movements are clipped as she greets me. She must suspect the reason for my visit, and my first move is to lend her my sense of calm, to reassure her that I'm here to understand her side of the story. I pull the blue banquet chair from the corner and place it near her desk. Keeping my tone light, I ease in, "How are your boys? The big game was last week, right?"

The thin veneer of rapport I'm trying to build crumbles as Erin's scowl floods crimson, and her back becomes rigid against her chair. Louder than I think she intends and laced with malice, she explodes, "I have been telling you for over a year that I needed help! I've been telling you repeatedly that this was a problem, and you offered NO support or solutions!"

My gut drops as if the floor has given way beneath me. This is not what I was expecting. A defense against her coworkers, sure. But not a finger pointed at me. Within an instant, my mind scrambles, chasing fragments of past conversations, desperate for proof that I hadn't failed her. The rebuttals line up in my head: *No, you have not been telling me this. You are being defensive and looking for any foothold to avoid responsibility. You're projecting your insecurities and failures onto me.*

Then it hits me. None of that matters. This was her reality, no matter what I think or feel. My role isn't to argue or correct, but to listen. To be a safe place for her to unload the weight she's carrying.

My defensiveness fades away as I lean forward, resting my hand over hers—chilled and frail beneath my palm. My voice is low and steady. "Thank you for letting me know how you feel. I can see you've been holding onto this for a while. That must have been hard."

She deflates like a popped balloon. Tears burst free as her whole posture slumps inward, and the fight drains from her. She barely chokes out, "You're not..." she lets out a sob, gulping, "...mad at me?"

I lean in more, voice warm and even. I assure her, "Of course I'm not mad at you, Erin. I appreciate that you are opening up and letting me know what's going on. It's not easy for me to hear this... but I want to."

Silence rests between us. Her tears ease, the battle abandoned, replaced by a fragile relief. A calmness washes over me too, gratitude overflowing for the steadiness that lets me meet her with understanding instead of reaction, and for the freedom of not being burdened by it.

This is a gift of empathy. When we aren't triggered by another's sharp words or rough delivery, we can pause to consider their perspective and move toward resolution and connection. Our own mental load and emotional impact are lightened.

The deeper this practice shapes me, the less I need to be right. The urge to win, prove, or defend quiets. Most often, it isn't even about me. I'm able to make space for resolution instead of escalation. That doesn't mean becoming a punching bag; it means staying steady so that I can identify the root of the conflict and create a chance for repair. Like with Erin, I'm able to defuse a situation before it creates division.

I wonder how that encounter with Trey might have unfolded if I'd been equipped with the empathy and perspective I have now. Maybe something like this:

The joy of the morning threatens to slip away when I read who was supposed to oversee the training last night. I'd rather stay in my showtunes-and-to-do-list cocoon, but I trust I can manage a basic conversation with Trey. No time like the present.

As I head upstairs, the math doesn't add up. *Wait. If he closed last night, why is he opening? Did he even go home?*

Over the clatter of the cooks banging pots and pans, I greet him. "Good morning, Trey! Didn't you close last night?"

Eyes down. "Yep."

I ignore the icy bite and try again, "Oh man, what time did you have to come in this morning?"

He doesn't even look up. "Early."

My hackles rise as I perceive his lack of eye contact and tone as rude, but I catch myself and wonder how I might sound with little sleep and feeling overwhelmed.

Catching the urge to be annoyed, I let it pass and ask instead, "You must be exhausted. I've got forty-five minutes before my first interview arrives. Anything I can take off your plate?"

With a slight shift in his stance and a weary exhale, he lists, "The chairs in the dining room need to be reset, and the Sysco rep will be here in ten minutes. Let him in and sign for the delivery."

Bristling at the absence of gratitude or cordiality, I remind myself I don't know the night he's had, and I can help with the tasks.

I assure him, "I'm on it!"

Later that day, I smell him before I see him. Cigarettes masked by cologne. Trey's sitting at the bar, studying the clipboard.

"How are you holding up?" I inquire.

His eyes lift from his notes. He doesn't answer. Just a flat, *what-do-you-want* stare.

I pull up a stool beside him, "That bad, huh?" I half-smile and nod toward his shoes. "Well, at least you still found a way to perfectly match your socks and tie. What's the story behind that anyway?"

He follows my nod down to his emerald chevron socks, then meets my eyes. *Is that a flicker of a smile?*

Empathy doesn't rewrite the past, but it does reframe it. It frees me from carrying burdens that were never really about me. It gives me the clarity to meet the next Trey, aggressive driver, or Erin, not with defensiveness, but with curiosity.

Over the years, people have countered, "I won't be disrespected" or "I won't let them speak to me that way." Empathy has given me a different kind of power. Leading with kindness and understanding in all aspects of my life is not accepting disrespect. No one can disrespect me unless I grant them the power to do so. Their words and actions belong to them. My response belongs to me. I can now perceive past the silent treatment, the reckless driving, the explosive emotions. It keeps me from internalizing it and helps me rise above the delivery and hear the true meaning behind the message, even when I can't relate or don't agree.

Some still object with, *"But feelings don't belong in the workplace."* Many argue that professionalism means leaving emotions at the door and powering through. But feelings show up whether I acknowledge them or not.

They walk in with every person, every shift, every meeting. Ignoring them doesn't make them disappear; it only blinds me to the forces driving the behavior.

I've experienced this not only in the workplace and in relationships, but also in the deepest corners of my past. While my childhood scars remain, evident in the tears shed while writing this chapter, I hurt for the adults who inflicted them. I now know some of their stories, their pain, their torment. I won't defend their behavior, and I do forgive them. I honor my younger self by extending empathy for what she couldn't yet have known. We all deserve grace for the gaps in our past understanding.

The truest value in pausing to see beyond someone's behavior isn't just what we give to others—it's what we also allow for ourselves. Recognizing we don't have the whole story lightens the weight of judgment, loosens the grip of resentment, and clears space for connection.

Empathy is strength. It's leadership. It's the superpower shift from being consumed by other people's storms to listening for what lies beneath the waves before reacting.

Sometimes, it begins with something as small and simple as asking about socks. May we all have a Kristen in our lives, teaching or reminding us to recognize the person first.

Some names and details have been adjusted out of respect for privacy.

DAYNE WHITEHURST

Dayne is a communication and leadership specialist who helps people become exceptional in how they connect, grow sales, and lead. Grounded in two decades' of experience in sales, education, and team development, she teaches precision communication and de-escalation strategies that align words with intention, build trust, and reduce mental load and emotional impact.

Passionate about helping people move beyond habitual interactions, Dayne empowers individuals and organizations to create authentic connection. As a coach and speaker, she equips audiences with practical tools and thought-shifting skills that transform everyday conversations into action, growth, and success.

She is currently writing two books: one revealing how to recognize and replace subtle language missteps that derail effectiveness, and another guiding workplaces and communities in mastering expert de-escalation practices that help others feel understood while preserving your own peace. Beyond her work, Dayne treasures adventuring with her husband and son.

linkedin.com/in/dayne-whitehurst
instagram.com/daynewhitehurst

9

THE UGLIEST WOMAN
IN THE WORLD

BY AVERY TOOMES

*T*he moment her face flashed up on the wall, I flinched.

God, she looks terrible, I thought to myself.

The woman's face projected onto the wall was swollen and her hair was a violent tangle of fried, berry-red strands. She hunched over herself, solemnly. She was completely disheveled, pulled apart, undone. Above all else, it was her eyes. I almost fell inside them, into the deep tunnel of grief that lived there. I couldn't hold her gaze. My eyes fled downward, seeking refuge, dropping to her shirt—to the faded Zelda tee I'd bought at Target three years ago. The fabric had worn soft at the collar from how often I wore it.

Wore. Wear. Wearing. She was wearing my shirt.

The air punched out of my lungs. The ruined face. The drowning eyes. *Me.*

Confusion swelled inside me before I came back to myself: the cold exam room, the TMJ specialist to my left, holding my hand, staring at me with abject concern.

"Avery?"

I was crying before I could stop it. All I could do was glance from the monster on the screen to the doctor and back again.

"That's me?" The words were mangled between sobs.

"Yes, Avery. That's you." She sighed as she tightened her grip on my hand.

"You're too young to be this tired." She let go of my hand and looked up at the projection. "You're too young to feel this old."

The sob that tore out of me didn't sound human. I folded into myself—red, brittle hair falling across my face like a curtain I could hide behind. *I know*, I wanted to say. *I know, I know, I know.*

I looked up at the doctor and shook my head.

"I used to be someone."

"Avery, you need to take a brea—"

"No, you don't understand. I used to have energy. I had a career ahead of me in New York. I had drive and ambition, and I was smart. I was . . ." My voice cracked. "I was beautiful. Really. And I didn't even appreciate it then, and now—" I pointed up at the projection. "Now I don't even know who that is!"

The monster was staring down at me now, almost mockingly. I found myself falling back into the empty world inside her eyes. I wanted to throw a chair at her face, to rip down the projector. I wanted to wake up from the nightmare that started nearly three years earlier.

The doctor sighed and went over the treatment plan again: my headaches were from my jaw pain. My jaw pain was from my misaligned jaw. My posture, exhaustion, and dizziness were all wrapped up in it too.

"I don't understand." my voice came out smaller than I intended. "I'm twenty-four. I was in the best shape of my life, and then I just woke up one day and it was there. The pain. Just . . . there." I could hear myself spiraling, but couldn't stop. "No family history. No accident. I never hit my head. We've been trying these jaw splints for months, and it's only getting worse. Everything is getting *worse*."

The doctor stood and turned on the lights. The face on the wall was still visible, but barely. A stain. A haunting.

"I think you need to see a psychiatrist." She paused. "You have a lot of mental health struggles that could be contributing to your pain. We've done everything we can, Avery. Based on what we've observed, we believe this pain is psychosomatic."

Psychosomatic.

The word landed like a fist.

All in your head. Not real. You're doing this to yourself. Your fault. A flash of doctors saying the same word rushed through my head. *Psychosomatic.* The word severed my connection to reality: if the pain wasn't real, if I was manufacturing it somehow, then I couldn't trust my own body, my own perception. Every sensation became suspect. Every symptom was evidence of my instability.

I left that appointment and drove home in silence. No tears. No screaming. Just the hum of the engine and the weight of my own breath. When I got home, I walked past my roommate without looking at her, closed my bedroom door, and lay down on the floor. The light moved across the ceiling in slow degrees. I watched it fade, then disappear entirely, until there was nothing left but dark.

Around four a.m., the pain woke me up, as it always did. I shuffled into the bathroom and turned on the light, squinting into the mirror.

There she was again. *Ugly*.

I turned my head back and forth, mushing and pulling on my skin. It looked like my face was in a funhouse mirror. A circus act, ready for the freak show. My brow bone was pushed forward, my nose puffy and wide, my jaw swollen on one side like I'd been punched. My eyes were sunken and wrapped in a purple hue. *Step right up*, I thought bitterly. *See the girl who turned her sadness into deformity*.

I couldn't look anymore. I turned away from the mirror and walked out to my kitchen. I stood in front of the open fridge, cold air washing over me. What would I consume to subdue how bad I felt? The leftover takeout I couldn't afford? The yogurt that had been sitting there for weeks?

Then I saw it: the wine bottle, half-empty from two nights ago when I'd tried to sleep through the pain. Today, it seemed almost magnetic. I reached for it without thinking.

I took the bottle to the bathroom and set it on the edge of the tub. I plugged the drain, turned the shower on, watched the water pool at my feet, and pulled off the same shirt I'd been wearing for three days. The water poured over me, hot enough to sting, and started filling the tub. I unscrewed the wine bottle and drank directly from it, not bothering with a glass. What was the point of pretending I had any dignity left?

The water raging down on me, the tub filling up ready to drown me, the cold, bitter liquid burning down my throat—it all felt like the universe was trying to tell me something. I wanted to wash away entirely. Dissolve. Disappear.

As I soaked, the bottle emptied, and the ever-present pain on the right side of my head began to numb. This was the cruelest irony: when I could finally get rid of the pain with substance or medication, I could grasp just how bad the pain actually was. It was a constant, swelling ache that had become the baseline of my existence. I didn't remember what it felt like not to hurt.

I started to cry. The tub started to overflow.

I didn't care. Water spilled over the edge onto the floor, pooling around the bathmat, probably seeping through the floorboards into my downstairs neighbor's ceiling. I didn't care about that either. *Let it flood. Let the whole building drown.* I thought about my car keys on the kitchen counter. I could get dressed, get in the car, and drive. Until the choice was taken from me. Until something happened. An accident. A cliff. An ending.

Or I could stay here. In this bathroom. With the water and the wine and the overwhelming certainty that I could make it all stop. That I could make the pain stop in a real, permanent way. It scared me how much I didn't want to live anymore. Not in a fleeting, passing way. This was standing at the edge and looking down, thinking: *Anywhere but here. Anything but this wreckage of a life and all my unfulfilled potential.*

Maybe they were right. *Psychosomatic.* The word echoed in my head. *It's all in your head. You're making yourself sick.* Maybe I was so fundamentally broken that my brain had decided to torture my body just to match the dysfunction within.

I turned the shower off with my foot once I realized I was really going to flood my bathroom, and reached for my phone on the counter. I sat back down, water sloshing over the tub's edge. My wet fingers left trails across the screen, smearing names as I scrolled.

"Hello?" Her voice was thick with sleep.

"Mom?" The word came out as a sob. I couldn't say anything else.

"Avery? Are you okay? What's wrong?" I could hear her sitting up in bed, suddenly alert.

"There's so much pain," I cried into the phone, my voice echoing in the small bathroom. "It's everywhere. It's consuming me. I don't even recognize myself anymore." My breath hitched. "It manifested physically and rotted me from the inside out."

"Didn't you see the doctors again? What did they say?"

"They said it's psychosomatic. They said that I'm doing this to myself. That it's not real." My voice cracked.

"Mom, I can't trust myself. I don't know what's real anymore. I look in the mirror and I see someone falling apart, but maybe I'm imagining it? Maybe I am crazy? I can feel the pain, but they keep saying it's not there, so how do I know? How do I know anything if my own brain is lying to me?"

I heard my father's voice in the background, muffled but clear enough: "Told you—"

"Don't," my mother said sharply, away from the phone.

"Mom." I tried to form the question I'd been too afraid to ask. "Did you ever feel this way? Like everything you've ever done, you've failed at? Like waking up is just harder than it is for other people? Like there's something inherently wrong with you?" The words were spilling out now, faster, more desperate. "I don't know what I've done. The pain is everywhere, and if I'm the reason behind it, then I need to go to a facility. I need help. Real help. I can't—" My voice broke. "I can't keep living like this. I don't think I'm going to make it through tonight."

"Oh, Avery, that's a little dramatic."

The words hit me like a slap. *Dramatic.* Of course. Even my suffering was too much, too performative, too *me.* At this point, I was a one-woman freak show of mass destruction. My pain was just another act for someone to sigh at and say that I had an affinity for theatrics, for high-drama exhibitoins of pain and suffering. To her, this was not a cry for help so much as an avant-garde performance piece no one asked to attend.

"Can you come up to Austin?" I asked quietly, my voice small now. "Please, I need someone here. I need help. I'm scared of what I might—"

"No, honey. We've got plans this weekend."

I heard my father's voice again, louder now, like he'd grabbed the phone or my mother had put me on speaker. "We've spent all this fucking money on those doctors, and she isn't better. What is it now, eight, nine doctors, Avery? And every single one of them has said the same thing—it's psychosomatic. At what point do you accept that they might be right?"

My jaw clenched reflexively.

"For three years she's done this," he continued, his voice rising. "It's always something. There's always a fucking problem."

I could hear my mom trying to shush him.

"No, call it what it is," he said. "She's lazy. She doesn't want to work. She is a disappointment to the point of *agony*. She got that degree to do what? Call us at four in the morning because she can't handle her life?"

The bathroom was silent except for the drip of water from the showerhead.

Drip.

Drip.

Drip.

"Mom," my voice sounded small and far away, like it was coming from someone else. "Is that true?"

"Is what true?" She sounded tired. *So* tired of me.

"Do you think I'm a disappointment?"

There was a pause. Long enough for me to know the answer before she said it.

"Not to the point of agony."

I hung up the phone.

The bathroom was completely quiet now. No drip from the faucet. No voices on the phone. Just me, drunk in a cold bathtub, in an apartment I couldn't afford, with a body I didn't recognize, and a pain no one believed was real.

I set the phone down on the floor and pulled my knees up to my chest, warming myself in the now-lukewarm water. *I was supposed to be someone.*

The next thought came clearly, calmly: *I'm not going to keep living.*

It was a fact. An inevitability. I couldn't keep doing this. *What is it now, eight, nine doctors, Avery? Three years.*

Thousands of dollars. And nothing. No answers. No relief. I was only getting worse.

Eventually, I pulled myself out of the tepid tub. I wrapped a towel around myself and walked to my bedroom, leaving wet footprints across the floor. I lay down on my bed in the dark and thought about the girl I used to be. The self that had more momentum than a bullet. I had been so marvelously determined. A force. *I used to be someone.*

My phone buzzed with a calendar reminder for my cardiologist appointment in the morning. I'd almost canceled it three times already. Another specialist. Another theory—postural orthostatic tachycardia syndrome this time. Another chance to be told it was all in my head. Number nine.

One more, I thought. *Just one more appointment. And if he says it's psychosomatic too, then you'll know for sure. Then you'll know that nine doctors can't all be wrong, that it really is all your fault, that you really are doing this to yourself.*

And then you can stop trying. The thought was almost comforting. An endpoint. A finish line. Permission to give up.

I woke up four hours later to the sound of my alarm drilling into my skull. My head was pounding—partly the wine, partly the ever-present pain. My tongue tasted like copper and regret. I dragged myself out of bed and into the shower again, washing off the wine and the shame and the lingering scent of desperation. I looked in the mirror after I got dressed and immediately looked away. Today was not the day to confront the girl in the mirror again.

The cardiology building was bland and forgettable, tucked off I-35. I sat in my car in the parking lot for fifteen minutes, forehead pressed against the steering wheel, willing myself to just go inside. *One more*, I thought. *Just one more dismissal and you can stop trying. You'll have your answer.* I got out of the car and walked toward the entrance, each step like I was wading through concrete. The automatic doors slid open with a soft whoosh, and I stepped into the air-conditioned waiting room.

The cardiologist's office smelled like antiseptic and old magazines. I filled out the intake forms: *yes to fatigue, yes to dizziness, yes to pain, yes yes yes to everything.* A nurse called my name and led me back. I followed her down a long hallway, fluorescent lights buzzing overhead, sending more pain into my skull. When we reached the small exam room, I sat on the paper-covered table and waited, pulling my arms around myself. I felt like I might shatter if anyone touched me.

The cardiologist was younger than I expected, with kind eyes. He introduced himself and began the usual choreography: blood pressure, pulse, stethoscope to the chest. I braced for it: *Your heart's fine. POTS isn't it. You seem anxious.* Then the inevitable referral to therapy, yoga, Jesus, or all three. *Psychosomatic. Number nine. Collect all nine and win a free lobotomy.*

But then—he paused.

He took off his stethoscope and sat back on his rolling stool, looking at me with an expression I hadn't seen from a doctor in three years: confusion. Not dismissal. Not pity. Not the barely-concealed frustration of someone who thinks they're wasting their time.

"Your heart is fine," he said slowly, like he was working through a puzzle in his mind. "Can you tell me about your other symptoms? Start from the beginning."

I laid it all out for him: the excruciating lack of sleep, the pain in my jaw and head, my fatigue, my dizziness, my depression, my anxiety.

He was quiet for a moment. Then he stood and stepped toward me, studying my face with careful attention. I wanted to disappear. I wanted to explain that I knew how ugly I was. That I used to be beautiful.

"Can I see your hands?"

I held them out, confused. He took them gently and turned them over, examining them.

"Have your hands and feet gotten bigger? Since all of this started?"

I almost laughed. "Yeah . . . I've gained weight."

"No, I don't mean weight gain. I mean have your actual hands and feet grown? Rings not fitting, having to buy bigger shoes?"

I stared at him. No one had ever asked me this. "I . . . yes. Actually, yes. I thought it was swelling from inflammation."

He nodded slowly, looking at my hands, then back at my face, his eyes moving across my features with that same focused curiosity.

"Your voice. Has it always been that deep?"

"I think so? I don't know."

He was quiet again. I could see him piecing something together.

"This doesn't make sense," he said, almost to himself. "You're twenty-four. You were healthy three years ago, and one day you just had all of these symptoms with no explanation?"

"I know it doesn't make sense," I said, my voice breaking. "That's why I'm here. That's why I've been everywhere. No one can figure it out, and I can't—"

"I believe you," he said. "I believe that you're in pain, Avery. I don't think it's psychosomatic."

Something in my chest cracked open.

Real. He said it was real.

I hadn't realized how desperately I needed someone, anyone, to validate my reality. To tell me I could trust myself. That I wasn't manufacturing this nightmare. That my body was really changing, the pain was really there, and I wasn't losing my mind.

"I need you to see an endocrinologist immediately," he said. "I'll send in a referral today. Can you get in this week?"

"Do you know what's wrong with me?"

"I think I do," he said carefully. "An endocrinologist will have to confirm. They'll run some tests: blood work, imaging. But if I'm right. . ." He paused. "If I'm right, this is treatable. All of it. The pain, the fatigue, the physical changes. It's not in your head, Avery."

I couldn't speak. I couldn't breathe. All I could do was sit there and stare at this man who had, in the span of twenty minutes, looked at me with curiosity instead of conclusion and found what eight other doctors had missed.

Three days later, my blood test came back only a few hours after the endocrinology appointment: IGF-1 at

900. Normal range was 100–200. They sent me for an MRI the same day. One hour in the machine, the rhythmic banging almost meditative after three years of chaos. Results would be emailed within twenty-four hours.

My mom didn't ask if she should come. She just showed up the next day.

We drove to Lady Bird Lake and found a bench under the trees. It was late afternoon, the water glassy and still. People jogged past. A dog splashed in the shallows. The world continued on while I waited to find out my results.

My mom sat next to me, not quite touching. We stared silently at the water. Then, my phone buzzed. *MRI RESULTS AVAILABLE – PATIENT PORTAL.*

My hands shook so badly that I almost dropped it.

"Do you want me to—" my mom started.

"No." I had to see it myself.

I clicked on the imaging results. A black-and-white MRI scan loaded a cross-section of my brain, ghostly and strange.

And there it was. White and round, sitting in the center of everything: a brain tumor.

"3 cm macroadenoma," I read aloud. "Pituitary tumor,

wrapping around the right carotid artery. The disease is called . . ." I stumble over the syllables. "*Acromegaly*."

I stared at the thing that had been living inside my head for years. Growing. Making *me* grow. Changing my face. Stealing my life. I Googled the word immediately: *acromegaly*, a rare disease caused by a benign tumor that secretes growth hormone. And there, in the search results, I saw her: Mary Ann Bevan. An English nurse who, a century ago, developed the same disease I had. She toured circus sideshows as "the ugliest woman in the world." The title I'd been giving myself for three years had belonged to her first.

"Oh, Avery," my mom said.

I didn't cry. I felt something closer to vindication and immaculate joy.

"It's real," I said. "Look! It's right there." I turned the phone toward her, showing her the tumor like it was evidence in my defense. "I wasn't making it up."

My mom stared at the image for a long time. When she finally looked up at me, her eyes were wet.

"I know," she said quietly.

We sat there in silence. Not the comfortable kind. The kind where too much has been said and not said, and neither of you knows how to fix it.

"You're going to need surgery," she finally said.

"Yeah."

"Brain surgery."

"Yeah."

Another long silence. A jogger passed. The dog kept splashing.

"I'm sorry I didn't—" she started, then stopped. "I should have—" She stopped again.

I understood what she couldn't say. That she was sorry, but also that she'd trusted the doctors, trusted the experts. How could she have known? That she'd failed me and hadn't meant to, and that both things were true at once.

"Not to the point of agony," I said quietly.

She flinched. "I didn't mean—" She took a breath. "I don't know what I meant. I was tired. Your father was—" She shook her head. "That's not an excuse."

"No," I agreed. "It's not."

I saw her: the guilt, the confusion, the love tangled up with failure. She raised me. She dismissed me when I was dying. Both things were true.

"I believe you now," she said.

I looked out on the water. "But you didn't then. When I needed you to."

"I know."

The words hung there between us.

"They'll fix it," she said. "You'll be okay." I heard the desperation in her voice. The need to believe that this story had a happy ending, that her daughter would survive, and that she'd get a chance to do better.

"I don't know that," I said.

The sun started to set, turning the lake orange and pink. Beautiful and indifferent to what was happening on this bench.

"I'm scared," I finally admitted.

"I know," my mom said. She didn't reach for me. She just sat there, holding the same fear.

"I'm still glad you came, Mom."

She didn't reply. The silence stretched, and my mortality sat between us, undeniable. I figured there was no better time to be honest.

"No one's broken my heart like you, Mom. No one even comes close." My voice cracked. "And there are days I want to be done. I practice it, you know? Not needing you."

She stared out at the lake, her face unreadable.

"It would be easier if you were all bad. With Dad, it's simple. He is who he is, and I stopped expecting anything a long time ago. But with you . . ." I could barely get the words out. "I shouldn't have had to be dying for you to show up for me."

She kept watching the water.

"And somehow . . ." My throat tightened. "You're still the first person I call."

She finally looked at me. Her face was lined with grief.

"I'm sorry," she said, looking away again to the lake. I let her apology hang in the air. I had no response. I didn't forgive her. I needed her. I loved her. All of it living in the same moment. Grief and love, sitting side by side, sharing the same bench.

The dog finally got out of the water, shaking itself dry. Its owner laughed and tried to dodge the spray. Life, continuing. Normal and strange and separate from us. I looked at the tumor one more time, then locked my phone. *It's not my fault.*

The following three days blurred together as I packed my life up and moved back to Houston, saw a team of neurosurgeons, got another MRI, and was scheduled for brain surgery the following day. I numbed into a ball of shock as they listed every bad thing that could happen in surgery, and how any of them could change my life forever.

The morning of surgery, I lay on my back, staring up at blinding fluorescent lights. My parents sat anxiously next to me, my mom holding my hand and my dad bouncing his knee. He had apologized in the way he always does, through a joke and a dismissive shrug. I didn't quite feel it. I didn't feel much of anything, though, as my parents said goodbye. I counted thirty-eight halogen lights as they wheeled me back to the operating room and lifted my body onto a cold, hard table.

"This is going to hurt a little," a male voice said. An electric pain spiked into my right wrist as he placed my arterial line. The man uttered something about a nice sleep.

"That would be nice," I muttered. My words slowed, and my eyes began to close. "I'm *so* tired."

The first thing I noticed when I woke up from surgery was not the tube down my throat or the nurses or my mother's face. It was the silence. The pain was gone. Completely, impossibly gone. Three years of constant agony, and suddenly nothing. Just quiet.

On day three, a nurse handed me my phone. "The doctors want you to take pictures. Your face is going to change rapidly."

I had not looked in a mirror since surgery. But on day

four, I made myself walk to the bathroom, flip on the light, and look.

My face was swollen from surgery, bruised beneath the eyes. But the other swelling, the distortion from years of excess growth hormone, was already retreating. My face was remembering itself. I took a picture. Then I pulled up the photo from the TMJ appointment, the projection of the monster on the wall from just a few weeks ago, and held it next to my reflection.

Before and after. Sick and healing.

The woman in that first photo looked ruined, eyes emptied out by grief. For three years, I had treated her like something to be ashamed of. I had called her ugly, dramatic, fragile, and failing. I had talked about her like she were not me. Like she was some grotesque impostor wearing my clothes.

But looking at her now, I saw the truth. She was a woman who was dying while everyone insisted she was exaggerating. A woman alone in a bathtub at four in the morning, trying to decide whether to keep living because she had been met with judgment over compassion. And even then, even at her lowest point, she kept going. Not because she believed in herself. Not because she was strong. But because some part of her, some part of *me*, refused to disappear.

Identity is strange like that. We tell ourselves that our remarkable self is the best, brightest version. The collected one. The impressive one. But sometimes the most ruined version of you is the one who kept the whole thing alive.

I looked at my reflection in the mirror, bruised, healing, and alive in a body that was finally quiet. The woman I had spent three years hating had saved my life. She had been here the whole time, keeping me alive until I was ready to return to myself.

I set my phone down on the sink with a soft click that felt like closing a door. Or maybe an arrival.

The woman in the mirror looked back at me, and for the first time in years, I didn't look away.

AVERY TOOMES

Avery Toomes writes the stories others are afraid to tell. This Texas-based writer, poet, and playwright transforms personal experience into powerful art that amplifies women's voices.

Her play *Your Power* sold out twice during its New York City debut and later ran in Philadelphia, confronting violence against women through an unflinching lens. The production dismantled silence and sparked critical discourse around the realities of women's lives.

A Pratt Institute graduate, Toomes works across writing, painting, and multimedia to create art that cuts deep and heals clean. She serves as Editorial Assistant at Sulit Press and as Assistant Editor at TRIBEZA magazine, while also writing artist profiles for Oro Art. Through her Substack essays, she shares the kind of raw honesty that helps women feel less alone.

Her work has also appeared in *Khrome Magazine, The Prattler,* and *Austin Woman Magazine.* As the chair of service and advocacy for the Zonta Club of Austin, she believes storytelling creates pathways for others to follow in finding their own voice and truth.

www.linkedin.com/in/avery-toomes
substack.com/@averylaaa
www.instagram.com/averylaaa

A WOMAN'S VOICE

BY LURLEEN LADD

J had just flown my entire team to Mexico because we had been unable to create a mission statement. We were a new group with a strong purpose: we knew that women artists over the age of forty faced sexism, ageism, financial inequality, resource fragmentation, and isolation from their peers—and we wanted to reframe what's possible. We called ourselves *Wavemakers Women in Music*. We had secured grants and funding right out of the gate, but we spent months debating the scope of our mission. Was it about the shortcomings of the music industry, or something much larger? We needed professional help.

We came to Mexico City to work with a marketing company specializing in social causes. Virginia, a lawyer who had studied and been a part of social movements in Central and South America, listened intently to me and my team. We described not only the perspectives of artists we'd worked with, but also our own experiences as women over the age of forty. Then, without warning, Virginia managed to sum up my entire life in one bold sentence:

"What you have created, Lurleen, is the exact intersection between music and women's rights."

Despite my carefully chosen business attire, I suddenly felt naked. My face flushed. I scrambled to fight back tears. How did Virginia understand my "why" so clearly? Her statement pierced deeper than Wavemakers. She seemed to speak directly to me, a woman who came "late" to a music career and who still harbored deep-seated doubts around my own self-worth.

Virginia had unwittingly held a mirror up to my life. And as I looked into it, the distortions began. Old doubts started to dance. Like Alice in Wonderland, I seemed to tumble through time.

First, the mirror drops me in the gym at St. Cecilia's Catholic School. I am wearing my PE uniform of navy shorts and a white shirt. Sitting on a bench next to the fastest runner in our fourth-grade class, I look down nervously. She is studying our thighs. She uses her hands to measure the width of her own and then compares the narrow distance to my chubby thighs pressing against the stretchy blue fabric. She laughs aloud and shows her friends.

I was one of two or three girls in elementary school who stood out in the worst way possible: I was a fat girl. Immediately and always a target.

Seeing myself as that little girl standing in her uniform, straining at the waist, the urge to pile on rises. "It's your own fault that she's making fun of you. Do not cry, it will just make it worse!" But before I can unload on her, I see her small hands fidgeting at her sides, the navy-blue sneakers with white shoelaces tangled like spaghetti at her feet. She is so small. She looks afraid, and I know why. School is not safe, but neither is home.

I was afraid every day, all day. My father was abusive and prone to explosions of temper and physical violence. His mood was very unpredictable, and he had a knack for terrorizing my sisters and me. He hauled us out of bed in the middle of the night if we left dishes in the sink. He saw any mistake or misstep as intentional and in need of a massive correction. He hit me with a belt when I was two years old because I opened the refrigerator and looked inside for too long. I was either the subject of violence or a witness to it. Whether it was myself or those I loved the very most, I was powerless to stop it. Silence was key. Speaking up only made things worse. A lifetime of hypervigilance was set into motion, and an unspoken mantra became deeply ingrained: *Just be quiet. Keep an eye out for trouble. Don't draw attention.*

I'm about six years old, standing in front of a white house with bright blue shutters in Jasper, Texas. My maternal grandmother aptly named her house Ginger Blue. It is springtime, and all the flowers are in bloom. I am standing with my grandmother, Marguerite Castro Sullivan. She is showing me fresh mint growing by the back door. I pick a leaf and bite into it. A cool blast of mint makes me smile. I am not afraid when I am with her.

My grandmother poured all the love and light she had into her family and community. She was my counterpoint to a scary world and a doorway to creativity. She had journals full of original poetry, photos, and memories of her many travels, dog-eared French fashion magazines, and silk-pointed toe pumps I clomped around in, trying to look like a lady. She was glamorous in a way that felt more like an invitation than a challenge.

In a large sun hat, dark sunglasses, and a scarf, she took me for long walks among the tall pines of East Texas, calling out the names of each plant and flower as we passed. Whether native or planted on purpose, she called them out. "Those are black-eyed Susans. And the ones with the tiny bouquets of orange flowers? Those are lantanas, or milkweed. They bring butterflies." Every path held a hidden world where fairies might live among the azaleas or the ground carpeted in pine needles. She imbued in me a sense of wonder and unending curiosity.

She was a trailblazer in her own right, seeking divorce from my grandfather, whose drinking ruined any chance of their long-term happiness. She did this in the late 1950s, when the price for her freedom hinged on custody of her children.

One Easter Sunday morning, after we had rummaged through our Easter baskets, I spied three untouched baskets filled with candy and toys in the front room. I assumed they were ours, but I was wrong. After mass, I saw my grandmother hand the baskets to a woman with two small children clinging to her legs. When I asked why she gave away our baskets, she told me, "That lady and her children are having a very hard time. They didn't have Easter baskets at their house this morning." When my grandmother gave her the Easter baskets, I saw her eyes fill with tears. Years later, I would learn that the woman and her children were refugees, and her husband was a violent alcoholic.

My grandmother was always quick to step in and help in small, quiet ways that exemplified women's power in the 1970s, just as the Women's Movement took hold. She, like many other women, worked behind the scenes, woman-to-woman, informally, lifting and guiding those in need to help and safety. Her empathy spoke volumes and galvanized my view of the world. I always knew she loved me just as I was, and she gave me the understanding that I, too, was full and capable of that kind of empathy. Though she never said it aloud, her message to me was clear: When you see others in pain, do something about it. Even small acts of kindness can be very powerful.

I was sitting at my desk in my new house in Austin, Texas. My husband, Dan, and I have returned after living out of state for his medical training. I supported our family as a social worker and then moved into healthcare administration. We had two small children, and now that all the training was over, our lives could finally begin. But instead of a new, easier path, I was very depressed. There was a gap forming. An old part of my life was dying; I just did not know it.

As the saying goes: depression is anger turned inward. I could not explain the anger. After over a decade of therapy, I believed the issues from my childhood were mostly resolved. I built my own family with intention, I had a successful career, and yet, that little girl with the tangled white shoelaces was still getting left behind. I know now, she was angry. All the joy and curiosity inspired by my grandmother had gone underground. I was all business and "just get through it" energy. But that approach had left me depleted and hopeless. I needed the empathy that I gave so freely to others for myself. I heard a distant voice inside my head asking for more.

As I sat at my computer, trying to journal through yet another day of feeling lost, I suddenly began thinking about music, something I always loved as a child. I was in dance and took piano lessons, but it was all lost along the way. I wondered, for a moment, what it would feel like to just sing. No plan—just do something that makes me happy. Voice lessons would be a way to start, but I immediately started to talk myself out of it. It was a sweltering August day, yet I was frozen at my computer. I could not bring myself to make the appointment. It felt like I had to choose: forward or backward. I looked at the grass outside, browning in the sun. The distant voice told me to make the appointment and to believe, like a cool fall breeze, something new was coming.

I'm in a crowded bar in Nashville, Tennessee, clutching a CD jewel case. That CD was a little miracle that contained three songs I had written and recorded. Shortly after starting voice lessons, I began writing songs. It happened without warning one morning. I was half awake when a melody popped up, and words followed. This part of my brain was like a rusted faucet in need of a shot of WD-40. Once it started, the music flowed.

Writing was one thing, but flying to Nashville to perform was a big secret. I did not want anyone to know. I assumed my friends and family would think I was crazy or delusional. I was almost forty, had no real training, and suddenly I was a singer-songwriter. It seemed as likely as becoming a prima ballerina or an astronaut.

Nonetheless, I attended the Nashville songwriting conference. The leader chose three attendees to perform at a local venue, and somehow, I was one of them. I still do not know how I ended up in that bar. I had barely gotten through the studio work; I was too nervous to even rehearse with musicians, yet there I was.

They call my name. I climb the steps and get in front of the microphone. I don't have cool clothes on, probably not even lipstick. The stage lights are hot on my face, and though I can't really see anyone in the audience, I know they are there. It feels like I am standing on the edge of a diving board over a pool of sharks.

The music starts, and I sing my song "Burn for You." Verse, chorus, remember the words, remember to breathe, here's that high note. The room is pulsating, but it's just my own heart beating, shaking my body. The song ends, and a voice from the darkness calls out, "You didn't suck! Do another one!"

I am on stage at Parker Jazz Club in Austin, the venue for the release of my second album. I have come a long way from that bar in Nashville, and I had struggled mightily with the part of me that wanted to stay hidden. That frightened girl from my childhood, whose nervous system never caught a break, needed my attention. She was always worried and afraid, and when I first started performing, she began to flare up. I tried to push through her fear, but each time I did, instead of it getting easier, the anxiety just got worse. Only when I found an amazing voice coach, Merrily Garrett, was I able to finally empathize with the terror I felt as a child. I was able to see the clear thread that linked my old wounds and my new voice. With support, I learned to listen to that frightened girl inside of me, but I kept performing, I kept writing, I kept recording, I kept singing. It was a hard-fought battle, and it took time. Eventually, I was finally able to allow my voice to give me strength, instead of reopening old wounds.

For the release of my second album, aptly named *No Goin' Back*, I wanted to feature other women like me for whom music was a lifeline. I worked with a group called NextTribe to publish my story about how I came to music at forty and made my way. I set up a contest for other women like me, over forty, to share their stories about music. The common theme in each story was the vital role music played in their lives. It saved them during divorces, the deaths of loved ones, job losses, bankruptcies, empty nests. Catastrophe after catastrophe overcome by their connection to writing and performing music. After reviewing all the applications, I flew two women to Austin to perform as my opening act for my album release.

This time onstage, I am nervous, but it feels different— more excitement than dread. The room is full of family and friends. I step onstage and speak into the mic: "I am still a work in progress." I will always remember that round of applause—not for my performance, but for being true to myself.

This moment was even sweeter because I was with the other two female artists. They each sang songs that resonated with my past. The first was "Me and Bobby McGee" by Janis Joplin. My mother and Janis attended Jefferson High School in Port Arthur, Texas. Having always felt a strong connection to Janis, I sang this song a thousand times when I was pregnant with my first child. I joked that she should've come out singing, "Freedom's just another word for nothing left to lose," when she was born. The second song was "Angel from Montgomery," in tribute to the amazing Bonnie Raitt. Artists building their work from their own experience and from the inspiration of other women: that was a map I could follow. Their stories are my stories. Connection is key.

Soon after the album release, I facilitated a Q&A for a women-in-music meetup. The stories of all the women from the contest still echoed loudly in my mind. During the Q&A, I shared statistics about how female artists struggle to book shows and are consistently paid less than their male counterparts. After another seasoned artist gave tactical information on pricing shows and booking gigs, the women in the room had a final request: they asked for everyone's email and phone number in the room.

Suddenly, it dawned on me. If I had assembled thirty-five plumbers or accountants in Austin, I guarantee that this group of professionals would have already known each other. Yet here were all these women, struggling in an industry with significant systemic issues, and they did not even have each other to lean on. And all this was compounded by feelings of being too old and too late to the game. If even the youngest artists feel unsupported and without a map, imagine my cohort of peers in an industry that values youth more than any other quality. These women feel consistently pushed off the stage and their work minimized. Is experience and skill worthless if the outside package does not look a certain way?

Wavemakers Women in Music was born out of my own experience and longing to connect with other women just like me. I saw the need, but was not sure I was qualified to push for change. There must be a more successful female musician who has played to stadiums of adoring fans who could lead the charge. Or it should be someone inside the music industry, like an agent or head of a record label. But when I looked around, no one was really speaking directly to women artists over forty in a concerted way. The more people I spoke to about Wavemakers, the more interest grew.

In 2025, we launched a grant for female musicians over age forty in the Central Texas area. At first, it was quiet, but the ping of each new application told us we were on the right track. Before the grant closed, we held a Zoom call to answer any last-minute questions about the application process. We were hoping just one woman would join us, but much to our surprise, ten applicants were waiting on the call. I will always remember the disbelief in their voices: "This grant is just for women over forty?" They couldn't believe it.

We were flooded with applicants. Much like the contest I held for my album release, their stories and videos showed lives dedicated to excellence in their craft and sustained by the joy and purpose music gave to each of them. They refused to give up even when the industry, band partners, or venues told them in not-so-subtle ways that, despite their talent and drive, it was time to exit stage right.

My team and I knew that to improve the music industry, we were going to have to innovate and find ways to support artists. It was vital to see their work as more than a commodity. While getting money into the hands of these artists was key, so was connection. Most of the respondents felt isolated as artists and without a comprehensive plan to guide their careers. The grant provided funds and coaching services as well as help marketing the artist's music and her own personal journey. The grant was titled "5 for 5 in 25"—five winners each received $5,000 in 2025. Of course, we could not choose just five winners. We ended up with six $5,000 grantees and an additional six winners of $1,000 for a total of $35,000 in grants awarded.

On the night of the awards, I met the women for the first time. When I came up to one winner, Alison Tucker, I thought of her story. She had followed the prescribed path all her life—doing what was expected of her but ignoring her own voice in the process. She applied for the grant to produce her first album of original work. As I went to introduce myself, I began explaining my background. She cut me off short and said, "I know who you are. I have done my research." She has a background in IT and has spent her career always getting the facts right. She said, "Lurleen, I see you." It meant so much, those three words: *I see you.* She understood who I was because of who she was. She knew we could come from diverse backgrounds, have different lives, and yet here we were. Together, united around music, and needing a path forward.

While I had hoped female musicians would embrace Wavemakers, I was surprised at how much our work resonates with women who are not musicians. I often joke about women being put on an ice floe and pushed out to sea once we are no longer of value, at the end of childbearing age. "I always knew I was supposed to sing from my diaphragm," I say. "I could not figure out what my uterus had to do with it!" Of course, it's not just in the music industry—this is just a part of outdated male supremacy and hierarchical systems that serve the few at the expense of the rest. I shouldn't have been surprised at how much our work spoke to all women.

We are all affected by the foreclosure of women's value.

Back in Mexico City, we conclude our meeting with a few statements that reflect Wavemakers' core beliefs: There's nothing more dangerous than a woman over forty with a voice. We absolutely fucking love women. When you are part of Wavemakers, you are never alone.

We ended with the most important statement of all: every woman has a story to share.

I began my story as a little girl afraid of the future, a future that was forever changed by the courage of my grandmother. I have evolved into a woman and an artist who understands the value of my own voice and the collective power of women to change the world. Women over forty resonate with power, sexuality, righteous anger, joy, and tenderness. Our happiness matters. Our voices matter. As the mirror was held to me, I hold that mirror to other women, an invitation to share their own voices, their own stories, with a world that needs to hear them.

LURLEEN LADD

Lurleen Ladd is a singer-songwriter, founder, and serial entrepreneur. She began her career in social work and transitioned into health care operations. Together with her husband, Dr. Dan Ladd, they built Tru-Skin Dermatology, a multi-site practice with over 100 employees. During their twenty-plus years of ownership, Lurleen co-founded The Shade Project, a skin cancer nonprofit that built shade structures at schools, co-hosted a medical call-in show on KLBJ, and was part of various nonprofits in Central Texas.

Lurleen began her music career at 40 years old. Through her own struggles in the music industry, she founded Wavemakers Women in Music to build community and economic opportunity for women 40+ in music.

Realizing the power of her own voice and that of all women over 40, she's turning up the volume on the power of women's voices everywhere.

wwimusic.com
Lurleenladd.com

11

WE'VE PAID ENOUGH

BY CIJI WAGNER

I froze.

The cityscape loomed outside the windows, the stone facades as cold and gray as I felt, tucked away in the corner. I blinked at the untouched bed, the camera pointed directly at my face.

"Do you need me to ask that one again?"

I wanted to scream that no one should be allowed to ask me that question. Instead, I nodded.

"What is something challenging you've had to overcome?"

Everything and nothing raced through my brain as I tried to string together the right words.

A competition-style reality TV show recruited me to interview for their upcoming season. To keep everything under wraps, I had to arrive at a hotel at the appointed time for the interview, text my contact, and they would let me know where to go.

I arrived that sunny, crisp late-winter morning and found a comfy armchair as I awaited my instructions. I scanned the room to see if I recognized anyone coming in for an interview amidst the flocks of tourists. I spotted one person as he scurried through the lobby, wild-eyed and fleeing, clearly having just interviewed. It was almost time. *Okay, Ciji. Breathe.*

A text alert buzzed on my phone: *Room 437.*

Wait, what?

They didn't rent a meeting room? Or a conference room? Going up to a hotel room to meet strangers was an impossibility. Alarm bells in my head started screaming at full volume. Was this a scam? Was something going to happen to me? Should I just leave now?

My heart raced as I drifted to the elevator, and my hands trembled as I pushed the button. I went into autopilot as I navigated to the room, knocked on the door, and entered.

No introductions. No pleasantries. No smiles. Just a demand: "Please tell us how to pronounce your name."

The two producers could have been me in another life. Twenty-something women desperately trying to prove themselves in a cutthroat industry. They directed me to a chair positioned in a corner that, if there was danger, would make a quick exit almost impossible. I was trapped.

"Why do you want to be on the show?"

I cemented my hypothetical escape plan: run into the bathroom, lock the door, and call for help. I bet they wouldn't be able to break down the door.

"Why should we cast you instead of someone else?"

With that settled, I could focus more on the interview.

"Can you describe your work style?"

I breezed through the next few questions. I had done enough TV segments to feel confident in my abilities.

And then: *the* question.

"What is something challenging that you've had to overcome?"

Just a few weeks prior, I sat in a dimly lit elementary school multipurpose room, listening to a lecture on hope, healing, and faith. The pastor preached about a story that I heard often enough to preach about it myself: a woman bleeds nonstop due to an affliction, and she believes that if she can get close enough to Jesus to touch his robe, she'll be healed.

That night, with the setting sun turning the room golden behind him, the pastor explained that this woman survived as a social outcast for thirteen years. She lived in isolation, with no hope of ever being accepted into society again. Never feeling whole again. Never being seen as clean again.

As I sat there, distracted by the scent of grocery store scones and cheap coffee, I thought, *Well, that would suck to deal with something for thirteen years with no hope of it getting better.*

And then—

The thought hit me like a tidal wave. *I have been dealing with something for thirteen years with no hope of it getting better.*

Out of nowhere, the memory of a sexual assault seared through my brain for the first time in over a decade. The shock and horror revealed a monster that had me bound, silenced, and desperate: The Big, Nebulous Pain. This thick, gray, putrid fog hung over me, pressing down, refusing to let me stand up straight, its tentacles constricting my breath.

The memory might have been hidden, but every part of me knew something had been wrong that whole time. My bones and my hair felt how this trauma threw my life off course. My cells and my soul recognized I had experienced something that decimated me. My skin and my organs radiated the pain that shook how I saw the world. Every part of me was saturated. All parts of me knew the source of my pain, but I couldn't remember it.

Over the next few days, the shame of not knowing what had happened nauseated me. It pulled at me every waking moment. My brain had done me the kindness of hiding the information until I had the ability to deal with it, but I was unglued nonetheless. I began falling apart at the seams, which were really just the mashed-together cracks that I had duct-taped and ignored.

The tape ripped as the wound reopened, and the pain oozed out. The decay that had settled into my soul was no longer contained, and the stench of it permeated every moment of every day... I couldn't escape it. It demanded to be acknowledged and would no longer tolerate being ignored.

I started to get a sense of what I had lived through, and it felt like the tears would never end. Something had broken open inside of me, and decades of pain flooded down my face, unstoppable.

I tried to hold it together long enough each day to get home and crash. I pushed myself endlessly to work better, harder, and faster all the time. I believed that if I could control everything in my life at every moment, then I wouldn't feel afraid any longer. That I wouldn't have to feel the weight of The Big, Nebulous Pain. I worked myself to injury, to illness, to hospitalization.

I tried to grasp just how bad things were, but the words and thoughts were slippery. Like a fish thrashing on the line, I couldn't hold onto them. Right when I thought I had put the right combination together, they would slide back into the abyss, lost to me again.

I ached to be known, to be understood. Everything felt like a question with no answer. I tried desperately to pin down these thoughts, to make some sense of my life. As I pulled, wrestled, and untangled, one thing became overwhelmingly clear: I would never feel understood if I didn't tell anyone what I had been through.

I selected someone I thought was safe to share my story with for the very first time. I invited them for dinner with the expectation that telling them my story would be part of the evening. With shaking hands, I typed up my story to read directly from the page, word for word, so I wouldn't have to try to figure it out in real time.

The time came, and I pulled out my pages to start reading. I stood in the corner of the room and watched myself at the table while I read aloud. I observed myself reading a story about my life that was so inaccessible that it could have been anyone reading a story about someone else, anywhere on the planet. Surely, it was not me, reading about the sheer pain and heartbreak in my own life. This was not my reality. This was the reality of another woman, in another timeline.

When I reached the end, I came back to myself and looked up, only to see tears streaming down their face. At first, I felt comforted. This person heard me and got what I had been through. *Finally*.

But then—

It quickly began to fall apart. They were overwhelmed by my story and could not regulate themselves. It was too much for them to hold. They knew what they had signed up for, and yet the burden was too heavy. The voice in my head confirmed my fear: that I was too much.

My shame magnified and intensified. The Big, Nebulous Pain fed on it, growing heavier, stronger, pushing me farther into isolation and desperation, its raspy whisper letting me know that I would always be alone. No one would ever understand me or even want to try. The lies about my unworthiness slithered into my soul.

I repeated this pattern, making deliberate attempts to share with people who were close to me. Over and over, I received a similar response—they could not hold it. It was too painful, too uncomfortable. They were often so shaken that I ended up comforting them, instead of the other way around. Trying to be understood left me feeling more isolated.

I no longer knew where to turn. The people in my life had proven unable to hold sacred what I had shared with them. The Big, Nebulous Pain enveloped me. I was cold, bound, and alone. Everyone was too far away, the walls too thick to break through. The chains were too strong to break.

Still, I kept at my quest. I attempted to share my story with those in my life, hoping, just once, to get a different response. Then one day, I shared it with a new roommate.

"Something like that happened to me too."

She then shared her own story. In that moment, it felt like the sun had parted the clouds. I felt a glimmer of warmth. Someone saw me—all of me—and she didn't turn away. She was able to hold my pain. Our threads wove together, linking us in a sisterhood that should never exist.

After that moment, I knew I had to create a group for survivors of sexual violence to be able to process trauma together. I was desperate for a space where I could talk about the worst things that have happened to me. A space where I wouldn't need to pretend that I was okay, where I wouldn't have to attempt explaining what they already knew.

This launched me into creating an eight-week workshop. Each time we met, we created something sacred; each participant committed to holding the burdens for each other. This was finally the space that I sought—not for answers, but to simply and beautifully be there for each other as we faced our pain. Together, we navigated the turbulent waters of our shared survivor experiences.

This workshop healed me in ways I never imagined possible. Part of me came back to life as The Big, Nebulous Pain loosened its grip on me. Those spaces were salve for the wounds that were still so raw.

But then—

The workshop ended, and we all drifted back to our normal lives. There was no clear path forward, and, honestly, no ability for any one of us to keep showing up with that level of intensity indefinitely. I made peace with our time together concluding.

In the midst of this, I came across two different people who had completed a type of therapy called EMDR, Eye Movement Desensitization and Reprocessing, but they didn't know how to explain it. I didn't have the space to investigate something that might be helpful that they couldn't explain.

Over the next several months, it became clear that my time in Washington, DC, was wrapping up. The city had become a symbol of the trauma I wanted to leave behind, and Austin called my name. While on the multi-day drive, I started reading *The Body Keeps the Score* by Bessel van der Kolk. I was immediately sucked in. It explained what EMDR was, the science behind it, and stories of people's lives being changed. People who had experienced significant trauma became free of PTSD.

Could it be—is it possible—what if—maybe that could be true for me?

While still on the road, I googled EMDR therapists in Austin and found the practitioner who would become my therapist. All it took was the consultation, and I immediately knew she was my person.

There was the typical history-gathering that happens with any therapy, but that's where the similarities ended. We began building my resilience—we created a place for me to put everything that felt like it was too much, where I could let these things sit until it was time to unpack them. Then, we created a place of peace for me to visit when I felt overwhelmed. At this point, I'll admit I wasn't entirely sold on EMDR.

On my way to my first session that would begin the reprocessing part of EMDR, I was almost involved in a car accident. I escaped being hit, pulled over, and ran to their leaking car. I helped them get out, called for the emergency crews, and sat with them until help arrived.

When I showed up for my appointment, I told my therapist about the accident, and she told me that it was natural to feel out of sorts over a traumatic event.

Traumatic event? What traumatic event?

I didn't understand why she was acting like I would be affected. I wasn't in the accident—they were.

The therapist gently explained that it was traumatic because of how close I was to being involved—my first taste of all that the word "trauma" encompasses. She said that we should do some reprocessing while it was still fresh.

She handed me two paddles, business card-sized and hunter green, their surface lightly textured. She placed them in my hands and turned them on. I felt a gentle, slow vibration. First in my right hand. Then my left. Right, left, repeat.

The directive was to recall the memory of the car accident I had just witnessed and see what else came up. Did I feel any emotions or have other memories coming to the surface? Within seconds, a second memory of an accident and a near miss I witnessed a decade prior came to mind. She gently urged me to go on.

The panic started to rise as I recalled the first time I drove after getting my learner's permit, the third memory in a set of traumatic driving experiences. A tractor-trailer nearly ran me off the road. My first experience as a permitted driver on the highway? A near-death experience.

My therapist asked, "What belief do you have about yourself connected to this memory?"

I didn't like the answer, but I knew it right away. "I can't trust myself to react correctly in dangerous situations."

Then, she calmly asked, "Ciji, what would you like to believe instead?"

I simply said, "That I can trust myself."

After about fifteen more seconds of vibrations, she clicked the machine off.

My heartbeat steadied, and the air filled my lungs without restriction. The fifteen years of car accident flashbacks faded away like they had never even existed at all. I no longer felt reactive when I thought about these memories. They weren't gone; they shifted and now felt benign, like any other neutral memory I had.

This ten-minute process illuminated a tiny fraction of what I carried while, at the same time, allowing me to put down this part of the burden, once and for all. EMDR sparked something within me that had been hiding to be brave enough to face the light. I finally had the courage and the resources to face it all. The very next session, we began untangling my trauma in earnest, beginning with the earliest thread.

As the weeks passed, I felt the anxiety melting away. I felt the burden lifting. The Big, Nebulous Pain no longer had the same hold on me. Its whispers no longer wormed their way into my soul—I could see them for the lies that they were. Instead of being a fish on the line, the words to express what I had lived through flowed to me like a river. The sharp edges of the cracks had been polished into a mirror that reflected progress.

Along the way, seemingly random memories would pop into my head, and I couldn't figure out why. At first, I shrugged it off. I was doing memory work; there was bound to be some odd stuff.

But one day, a memory came to mind that I sat with a little longer than the others. I tried to untangle this elusive knot. *Why this memory? Why now?*

Then it hit me: *This memory wasn't some "not great" situation in my dorm room. It was another assault.*

I went through the Rolodex of memories that had recently crossed my mind:

Oh, that wasn't just a bad day at work. My coworker intentionally injured me. That was abuse.

It wasn't a misunderstanding. He manipulated me to benefit financially.

A message at church that didn't quite resonate? Of course, it was spiritual and religious abuse.

The sexual assault that suddenly came back to me, sitting in the multipurpose room that day? That was just one day in a years-long abusive relationship.

As I pulled the thread, I saw how abuse and harm underpinned every area of my life. Each time I untangled one part, something new revealed itself.

Once I started seeing it, I couldn't unsee it. Once I gave my brain permission to process, it ran full speed, connecting the dots in rapid fire. Exhausted, I wondered how much more I could handle. *How much more could there be?* The awareness fatigue was becoming debilitating with what felt like a fresh, miniature hell to work through with each new connection.

Once I pulled the thread, I revealed a tapestry full of knots, torn strings, and disorienting patterns. I wasn't living the stable, consistent life I thought I was. Getting a bigger picture made it clear it was far more than just these few instances of sexual violence that drove me to EMDR in the first place. I had to burn everything I knew down to the ground and start from scratch.

I lived in a contradiction. For the first time, I understood that The Big, Nebulous Pain was so big and nebulous because of the intensity, breadth, and duration of harm I had experienced. At the same time, EMDR allowed me to experience freedom in ways I had never known before.

About eight months in, I completed an EMDR session that was particularly impactful. A few different threads we had been working on finally came together, and the picture became clear. For years, I had been hunched over, protecting my heart from the world, but now, I could stand up straight and hold my head high. It felt like magic.

On the way home from that appointment, I steeped myself in this feeling of healing and vitality I had never known before, knowing my life would be different from this point forward. And then, I felt something I didn't expect: anger.

Anger that it was costing me so much of my time, my energy, and my money. *Why was I paying for this?*

I couldn't afford it. I pulled money from my savings each week with the faith that this investment was one worth making.

If I was willing to give so much of my time and my energy, why did I have to give my money too?

Shouldn't he have to pay for this?

Shouldn't someone else have to pay for this?

Haven't I paid enough?

I became angry when I thought of all the other survivors I knew, people who had dealt with the worst life has to offer, and they had hope for the first time that something could work for them, too. But, they couldn't afford it either.

Haven't all survivors paid enough?

The answer is yes. We have all paid enough. I would figure out how to secure funding for survivors to access EMDR. I didn't know what that meant or what that would even look like. I just knew I was going to do it.

Within three weeks, I had founded a nonprofit organization, Louder Than Silence, that would do this very thing. I was still getting EMDR myself, but I knew with my entire being that this would change other survivors' lives too.

Louder Than Silence began by offering EMDR, but it quickly became apparent that the backbone of this work lies in a group of survivors supporting one another as they navigate their trauma. I quickly folded the workshop I had previously done into our programs. From there, we've added a whole range of community-building activities to keep people connected and supported.

Over the past seven years, we've provided over 700 EMDR sessions. We've had nineteen cohorts of people start our programs through our twelve-week workshops. We've amassed thousands of touchpoints that can't all be tracked—the texts, the calls, the emails, the coffees. We have a group of eighty-five people who have looked their trauma in the face and said, "I won't let this ruin my life anymore." And, I am proud to say that all of this has been offered at no cost to participants.

Because, as it turns out, survivors really *have* paid enough.

It's been both a joy and a tremendous heartbreak to walk alongside other survivors facing these wounds. I've witnessed lives change in ways that were beyond the reach of even my wildest dreams.

At Louder Than Silence, we've created several staff positions for community members. We've seen survivors return to school and earn degrees. One community member even became an EMDR therapist herself. We've seen people start businesses, end harmful relationships, and pursue legal action. We've seen families formed, joy returned, hope rekindled, life restored.

Of course, my journey didn't stop when I launched Louder Than Silence. I kept leading workshops, completed EMDR, launched new programs, and began doing bodywork to release the trauma physically.

The Big, Nebulous Pain melted away into a river, one that allowed others to cool themselves from the harsh reality of their pain. It gives all of us abundantly more life as we drink it in. And then, as their own versions of The Big, Nebulous Pain melt, they offer the same to the people in their lives. It compounds as it grows, reaching the lives of thousands of people because each of us has committed to this healing work.

Over the years, when I've spoken with others who have completed EMDR, I've heard numerous stories from people who recognize that the life they have built for themselves was previously unimaginable, that the gratitude still hits them for all the pain they no longer carry. They celebrate the wins of showing up for themselves and others, embracing the fullness and messiness of humanity.

I still catch myself in those moments, peace flowing from the scars that are no longer open wounds—when I'm reading a good book, snuggling with a puppy on the couch, digging in the dirt in my garden, or when I feel rested and refreshed when I wake up in the morning; when I'm doing meaningful work or sharing a thoughtful meal with someone I love. I drink in these moments because they were hard-fought. I allow my heart to stay open to the beauty around me because I am no longer chained to The Big, Nebulous Pain.

It's now been a decade since that first memory was unblocked. I have built a life for myself filled with light and peace and purpose, where there was once a desperate grasping for anything to hold onto. I live a life that could never have existed while I was in survival mode—a life that I can simply and beautifully describe as "good." It still feels like magic.

But if I'm honest, the question still haunts me: *"What is something challenging that you've had to overcome?"*

Looking into the eye of the camera in that hotel room, I lied. I was not prepared to bear my tender soul to the world yet.

But if I could do it over today? I know how I would answer.

"How much time do we have? That's how I'll know where to begin."

CIJI WAGNER

Ciji Wagner is the founder and CEO of Louder Than Silence (LTS), a nonprofit that provides long-term care, community, and resources for survivors of sexual violence, all at no cost to participants.

With a degree in Baking and Pastry Arts and a background in hospitality, Ciji worked in various roles in the restaurant industry before entering the nonprofit sector as an executive chef. Since that pivot, Ciji utilized her expertise in managing businesses to launch LTS in 2018.

Over the course of her career, Ciji has offered over 150 trainings and presentations on multiple platforms such as live and recorded television, podcasts, conferences, guest lectures, and other in-person events. Ciji brings her calm and engaging presence as she speaks from years of personal experience, coupled with her unique ability to explore a topic deeply and then share her knowledge in a way that's easy to understand.

www.louderthansilence.org
www.instagram.com/louderthansilenceorg
www.youtube.com/@louderthansilenceorg
www.cijiwagner.com

EMPATHY IS ACTION, NOT ABSTRACTION

BY HILARY GRAHAM

That Monday morning, before we boarded our flight from Austin to Denver, the first domino fell. Reductions in force were nothing new, but this occurred in an unexpected place: an airport business lounge. This was step one in a triad of corporate exits about to unfold over the next several days. As I stepped out of the Denver airport into the hot, dry summer air, I braced for the week ahead. Sliding into the back of the Uber, a quiet sense of impending relief washed over me —the wheels were already in motion.

On Tuesday afternoon, my general manager and I walked into an auditorium filled with sales professionals from my company. I announced a change to the agenda, then stepped aside as he took the stage. I've launched countless meetings—but this one felt different. My hands moved slower, my awareness sharper. The weight of the moment was undeniable.

Waves of emotion broke over the auditorium as a composed leader delivered news that profoundly shifted the career trajectory of everyone in the room. In a single moment, the atmosphere transformed from a vibrant, focused learning environment to a cacophony of loss and confusion. As I looked out, I saw three women sitting beside each other with tears streaming down their faces. A man was pacing while releasing unsettling guttural groans. To my right, a couple of feet away, one woman asked another for clarification. Had she heard the announcement correctly? The business was being sold.

The sale of a business may close with a few digital signatures, but behind the transaction, I was witnessing the very real human experience of an organization letting go. Having grown up in earthquake country in southern California, I know that seismic shifts are never predictable, but they are inevitable. The challenge for business leaders is to extract clarity from disruption, distill lessons into principles, and translate them into intentional action.

As I prepared for the summer of 2025, I anticipated the familiar rhythm of commercial meetings. After nine years leading marketing in healthcare, this was far from my first rodeo. Each fiscal year, our sales teams came together to align on priorities. It was deeply energizing to develop diagnostic tests that inform moments that matter in people's lives, whether helping bring a new life into the world or detecting cancer early. I have the privilege of driving meaningful health outcomes while delivering measurable business performance—a rare intersection of purpose and impact.

What I didn't anticipate was that months of planning would result in a single week where three common corporate events unfolded in uncommon succession: a reduction in force on Monday, the announcement of a business line divestiture on Tuesday, and a structural reorganization of the commercial team on Wednesday—culminating, finally, with a wellness retreat on Thursday.

Pattern recognition has always been one of my superpowers. I've found that when events converge with such a quick cadence, it creates a clarity that makes interpreting a pattern and extracting meaning more evident. This week crystallized my own management mantras: Lead with Kindness, Live with Abundance, Manage with Intentionality, and Empathy Is Action.

Through these principles, I've learned that empathy in corporate leadership is the capability to accurately understand and anticipate the perspectives, emotions, and motivations of others, and to use that insight to guide communication, decision-making, and action. It goes beyond awareness—it's about applying perspective-taking to build trust, strengthen collaboration, and enable higher performance—especially when the actions required to achieve the desired result are hard. I learned that empathy isn't an afterthought; it's woven into the DNA of my professional life, and beyond.

Lead with Kindness

I was leg pressing 370 pounds with my trainer when I first learned about radical honesty. My trainer is not who you might expect: she has a master's in environmental science from Duke, and our conversations always meander through a gamut of surprising topics. One day, as I focused on breathing against the weight, she told me about Brad Blanton's *Radical Honesty*. I was fascinated. It's not about brutal bluntness—it's about courageous, intentional communication that creates trust and drives sustainable performance across people and projects.

As I learned more, I realized that *nice* and *kind* are often used as synonyms, but they're not the same. *Nice* is often about surface-level harmony: avoiding conflict, softening feedback, and prioritizing short-term comfort over long-term growth. Being nice can come at the expense of clarity, accountability, and progress. *Kind* is grounded in respect and empathy, but paired with honesty and courage. Kindness means delivering feedback directly, setting clear expectations, and making tough calls when needed—because you care about people's growth, the team's health, and the organization's success. Nice preserves comfort. Kind fosters harmony and growth. I realized softening conversations comes with a cost.

I had two team members at loggerheads. One person had tremendous intellectual horsepower, but their brilliance manifested as unnecessary complexity and strife. The other was great interpersonally, but repeatedly arrived unprepared for high-profile meetings. Coaching conversations were abundant, but they were more like Band-Aids than solutions. It was a recipe for diminished collective performance and a far-reaching, dysfunctional culture.

We are often socialized to soften difficult conversations, but in reality, being clear is kind. Clarity is direct, concise, and understandable. I was not clear to these two team members that their complexifying behavior and underperformance were unacceptable and would result in their separation from the organization.

I realized I had been leading my team to be nice, all while operating from a scarcity mindset and failing to proactively address mismatched team members because I was afraid that I might not be able to backfill their positions. It's a disappointing and uncomfortable truth—especially for someone who genuinely believes that people are my passion. Leadership requires more than niceness; it requires intentionality, clarity, and the courage to make decisions that elevate the team as a whole.

I never acted, and I regret that deeply. Instead, the problematic individuals were exited during that week in Denver. What troubles me most is the contradiction: I've always prided myself on shielding my team from external pressures, yet I allowed this internal strain to persist. I failed to realize that by being nice, I was actually being unkind—unkind to the individuals I wasn't direct with, and unkind to the broader team that bore the consequences of my inaction. Empathy doesn't mean avoiding truth; it means having the courage to deliver it in a clear way that respects the other person's humanity and potential. It was my job to make a hard decision, to step in, to learn when and how to let go.

Live with Abundance

I was pregnant, flying home from California after another week of cross-country commuting, sitting in the very last row of the plane.

I had imagined pregnancy as a magical, glowing chapter in my life. In reality, it reflected my lived experience, rooted in science and self-advocacy. My pregnancy was the result of medical art—an intrauterine insemination. Two weeks after that milestone, my then-husband came home early with news that he'd been fired. It was a triple shock: I had just learned I was pregnant with my first and only daughter; he had hidden his struggles at work; and I had just stepped into a demanding new sales role that required weekly travel. I was now the sole income for our growing family, but even my job was tenuous given my impending maternity leave.

On that flight home, I watched men offer to lift bags for other women, but not for me. Throughout my life, I've projected strength—whether through physicality, personal presence, or professional confidence. That signal has often been protective, even empowering. But in that moment, I realized something: signals of strength don't mean we don't crave support. Sometimes, strength and vulnerability can coexist.

I put in my earbuds and started to listen to Viktor Frankl's *Man's Search for Meaning*. Knowledge is power, and this is my go-to move when I'm struggling: get information from a variety of sources to triangulate a solution. Frankl was a Jewish psychologist and wrote his book just one year after being liberated from a Nazi concentration camp. A profound lesson from his writing is that we cannot control circumstances—but we can control our responses. Freedom lies in choosing our attitude, even in the harshest conditions.

I took this lesson from the back row of that airplane and began to use it to examine my professional life. What I find most striking, in retrospect, is the contrast between my personal and professional outlooks. In my personal life, I embraced an abundance mindset—projecting strength, trusting in possibility, investing in relationships, and focusing on long-term growth. Yet professionally, I had slipped into patterns of scarcity thinking, unaware of how deeply it was shaping my decisions and limiting my team's potential.

An abundance mindset is the belief that there are enough resources, opportunities, and possibilities for everyone to succeed. Leaders with this mindset focus on collaboration, trust, and empowerment. They make decisions that elevate both individuals and the organization, proactively invest in people, and see challenges as opportunities to expand impact rather than threats to protect against.

A scarcity mindset is the belief that resources—time, talent, money, or opportunities—are limited. In leadership, it can manifest as avoiding difficult decisions, holding onto underperforming team members, or resisting collaboration, which ultimately constrains growth and innovation. A scarcity mindset narrows empathy because it's constrained by fear of "not enough."

In my work, I've experienced two very clear poles of the spectrum between scarcity and abundance. I call them *collaboration drag* and *the power of pulling together*.

Picture this: One draft horse can haul an astonishing 8,000 pounds on its own. Common sense would suggest that adding a second horse simply doubles the output to 16,000 pounds. But in reality, two horses working together can move 24,000 pounds—three times the weight of a single horse. Even more remarkable, when those same two horses are trained side by side and learn each other's rhythm, their combined strength can reach 32,000 pounds. That's four times the load either could manage alone.

This is more than an interesting fact about horsepower—it's a vivid lesson in the power of alignment. It's not addition, but multiplication, also known in business jargon as *synergy*. A team of talented individuals doesn't automatically translate into breakthrough outcomes. Just as two draft horses need time to train together, employees need shared goals, clear communication, and trust to multiply their impact. Teamwork isn't addition—it's multiplication. The most powerful business teams aren't built by stacking the biggest resumes in one place. They're built by aligning strengths, balancing personalities, and finding a rhythm where the whole works as one. This is the power of pulling together.

However, teamwork can sometimes have the opposite effect. Like draft horses, when people pull in different directions, energy is wasted and progress stalls. On paper, a team of five should deliver the work of five. But that assumption breaks down the moment one member consistently underperforms or creates interpersonal friction. Instead of contributing, that individual subtracts from the group's collective capacity. This is collaboration drag.

I first experienced collaboration drag while working with the internal marketing agency at my company a few years ago. The leadership of the agency wasn't aligned with core company values, which resulted in poor hiring decisions that led to high turnover. Employees on my team, for example, had an average tenure of 41 months, but the marketing agency only had 10 months. My team was adversarial to the entire agency team, knowing they were likely transient, and we assumed they had negative intent.

The struggle came down to one thing: approaching head count from a scarcity mindset. From our perspective, headcount seemed to be related to power and optics, not outcomes achieved by the team. When leaders hold onto headcount and worry about how the work will get done with a smaller team, the damage compounds. Productivity slows, trust erodes, and the team suffers. But choosing to exit a problematic employee and compose a team with complementary strengths—even if it's a smaller team—can reset expectations, lift morale, and elevate the entire group's performance.

Scarcity distorts our mental math. Acting boldly with an abundance mindset not only strengthens your team but also unlocks the capacity you already have. The equation to optimize success always requires realignment—and sometimes involves subtraction. Now I realize that living with abundance isn't linked to the actual amount of resources. It's a mindset. In the current resource-constrained environment, I could choose to focus on all that we don't have and can't do. Instead, I've chosen to use the resource constraint to focus on the highest-impact investments and deploy my team and budget against those priority projects. Ultimately, mindset frames lived experience more strongly than the reality of the resources available.

Manage with Intentionality

In Texas, we've experienced several brutal winter freezes over the past few years, a new environmental reality. One of the most vivid experiences during these times was hearing tree branches heavy with ice shearing off and explosively falling to the ground, often causing collateral damage. Since then, I've become more intentional about pruning my oak trees to ensure they stay healthy and resilient, not overburdened by weight they cannot bear.

That image of pruning large oaks always brings me back to a different kind of tree—the bonsai. Bonsai cultivation is a master class in intentionality. Every cut, every wire, every choice is made with a long-term vision in mind. Growth is shaped, not left to chance. Intentionality transforms potential into something impactful.

I had the ambition to become a VP of marketing by age forty, so at thirty-six, I crafted a plan to gain the two critical experiences I needed to get there: profit and loss responsibility and a successful product launch.

At my company, a leading manufacturer of diagnostic instrumentation and reagents, I saw an unmet market need for custom assay services. With limited resources, I made the case, secured a talented team member, and together we carved out space—literally and financially—to make it happen. Demand grew, revenue followed, and the business scaled—profitably. Profit and loss experience: check. Next, I turned to product development. Although that responsibility traditionally sat within R&D, I brought deep customer insight from years in content marketing, where I told the stories of our customers' breakthroughs. Those relationships gave me access to their unmet needs and pain points. By bridging that understanding into the product development core team, I helped shape and launch a next-generation instrument. Product launch: check.

These successes share a common thread: fierce customer centricity—empathy in action. I listened intently to our customers, understood their needs, and became the conduit that translated market demand into organizational strategy and action. At age thirty-eight, in the heart of the coronavirus pandemic—BOOM—I landed the VP role. But while intentional growth and strategic execution became the throughline of my leadership journey, there were blind spots in applying these tenets to intentionally shape my team.

For a time, I believed retaining team members who did not reflect my performance expectations was simply a matter of extra coaching or patience. What I didn't see was that these team members were taking an even bigger toll than I realized: the erosion of my team's brand. My job as a leader was not to coach these team members into work that wasn't suited to them; my job was to ensure I had the right people on the team in the positions that best applied their professional and personal skills.

That insight sharpened further at a corporate celebration honoring colleagues with more than twenty years of tenure. With a plastic cup of champagne in hand, gazing at a line of bobblehead dolls in white lab coats, I listened to the managers give toasts to each of the folks with these exceptional runs of corporate longevity, each toast punctuated by applause. I heard two themes woven through every story: embracing change and excellence in tradecraft. Those qualities enable people and organizations to grow together with intentionality.

Embracing change is essential to sustaining meaningful relationships and high-performing teams. Relationships —whether personal or professional—are never static. Over time, you are either growing closer or growing apart. You cannot remain with the same person or organization you were with twenty years ago; they have changed, and so have you. Just as with oak and bonsai trees, change is the only constant. But embracing change does not mean avoiding discomfort. High performers distinguish themselves by acknowledging the emotions that come with change, sitting with them, and moving through them deliberately, often more quickly and effectively than others—turning transition into growth and opportunity.

Tradecraft, too, matters. It is the specialized skill and know-how that defines expertise. In some fields—medicine, law—it comes with accreditation. In others, like sales or marketing, the bar to entry may be fluid, but true mastery comes from understanding foundational principles and committing to continuous improvement. High-performing teams apply their unique tradecraft to advance organizational priorities, flexing their skills where they're needed most.

That evening's celebration reinforced an obvious truth: proactive talent management builds cohesion, elevates performance, and sustains culture over time. I left this celebration of toasts with a personal commitment to be intentional about performance management moving forward.

That commitment was soon tested. I inherited a team member who was well-liked personally but whose skills no longer matched the needs of the organization. She struggled with change—an allergy to adaptability that was incompatible with high performance. We are the captains of our own careers, and without intentional alignment, momentum happens *to* us rather than *because* of us. This time, I acted decisively. With these clear signs of misalignment, I chose to proactively manage and transition her out. Despite all the recent changes and difficulties, I knew it was the best decision for the team, and it was my job to perform it with intentionality.

Intentional leadership is about shaping outcomes, not leaving them to chance. The health of a team, and the strength of its brand, depends on it. And as a commercial leader, I would argue that intentionality is most effective when it's empathetic and responsive to our customers' needs. Like pruning oaks or cultivating bonsai, it requires courage, discipline, and a clear vision of what you're building.

Empathy Is Action

My team was still absorbing the impact of three unexpected corporate exits on Monday, Tuesday, and Wednesday, but Thursday marked a shift. My team made a deliberate choice: we would close this week not with quotas or directives—as is customary—but with a wellness session. At the time, it was simply an expression of our belief that sustained high performance requires intentional care for our people. We couldn't have anticipated just how powerful that decision would prove to be.

Sage, my manager and the division's commercial leader, is a true Renaissance man: former professional basketball player, father of five, devoted husband, political science major turned athlete turned healthcare executive. While his résumé impresses, what stands out most is his profound, holistic care for people and his ability to extract and share meaning from life's most challenging moments with unflinching honesty.

That day, we listened as Sage, standing at six-foot-ten, tears in his eyes, shared one of the most defining moments of his life—the death of his newborn son. As Viktor Frankl taught, life's lows can be devastating, and the loss of a child is among the most profound. As Sage recounted losing his son just days after birth, he posed a challenge to us: if a life so brief can leave such an impact, what impact can you make with yours? He modeled empathy through storytelling—vulnerable and brave, never indulgent. He offered lessons drawn from personal experience to help our team confront our recent difficult moments, connecting with authenticity while respecting boundaries.

I've worked with Sage across two companies for eight years collectively. He is the most influential embodiment of empathy in action I've ever experienced. I tend to operate with kinetic execution, while he masters the nuances of the human condition—offering wisdom on relationships, conflict, and complexity, always with curiosity and timeliness to minimize escalation.

During my performance review, Sage offered a striking piece of coaching: *calm your mind*. He cares about me as a holistic human and wants me to thrive, not only as the marketing leader of our division, but also in all personal roles I play. It wasn't about just goals or metrics. It was a deeply personal reminder that empathy includes seeing the human first, the professional second.

In the late 1970s, neurologist Antonio Damasio studied a patient he called Elliot. Elliot had undergone surgery to remove a tumor from his prefrontal cortex. Afterward, he was still highly intelligent—his IQ, memory, and language skills were fully intact. But he had lost something essential: the ability to feel emotions. Elliot could analyze situations endlessly, but he couldn't decide. He would spend hours weighing trivial choices, get lost in irrelevant details, and fail to move forward in everyday life. His case became the foundation of Damasio's somatic marker hypothesis—the finding that emotions aren't a distraction from rational thought; they're the very mechanism that makes decision-making possible.

This lesson matters for leaders today. Too often, empathy is dismissed as a soft skill—something "nice to have" but not essential. Elliot's story proves the opposite.

Without emotional signals, intelligence alone can stall out. Empathy is what allows us to cut through noise, read the human context, and act decisively. Empathy isn't passive. It's an active discipline: noticing when someone is struggling, asking the harder questions, stepping into discomfort, and making decisions that honor both people and outcomes. It's not softness; it's a catalyst for clarity, alignment, and progress.

Especially in biotech and healthcare, empathy is far more than a soft skill—it's a strategic capability. The products we bring to market matter, but how we bring them forward, with empathy in action, matters just as much. When we lead with empathy, we design and communicate on both rational and emotional levels, bridging innovation in the lab with impact in the clinic.

The truth is, we are experiencing the human condition all the time. While many of us consciously compartmentalize how we show up at work versus at home, authenticity and vulnerability are the foundation of meaningful connection, trust, and lasting impact. As Sage modeled, empathy, at its core, is action. It lives in the questions we ask, the attention we give, and the care we embed in both the extraordinary and the ordinary moments. As I often say, people are my passion. And when we elevate people, we elevate performance. When we lead with empathy in action, the ripple effects extend far beyond ourselves, shaping teams, organizations, and the patients we ultimately serve.

By leading with intentionality and empathy in action, I navigated a week that began in loss but ended anchored in connection, meaning, and forward momentum. Pattern recognition has always been one of my superpowers, and I can't help but notice how the elements of that turbulent corporate week now echo through my personal life. The mantras I've carried into leadership—kindness, abundance, intentionality, and empathy—have taken on a deeper weight. They're no longer just words on a slide or phrases to inspire a team. They've become embodied actions, principles I choose to live by across all areas of my life.

HILARY GRAHAM

Hilary Graham, PhD, MA, is a storyteller and strategist passionate about helping people get better answers in moments that matter most to their health. As Senior Director of Marketing for Bio-Techne's Diagnostics Division, she leads portfolio strategy, product management, and marketing while serving as commercial chief of staff. Her career spans diagnostics and life sciences, including leadership roles at Luminex, Syneos Health, and MD Anderson Cancer Center.

Hilary's superpower is connecting the big picture with the smallest detail. She blends strategic vision with empathy, creating clarity and alignment that drive meaningful, lasting results. Known for her transparent and inclusive leadership style, she builds high-performing teams and energizes those around her. A fearless force of nature, Hilary brings curiosity, creativity, and joy to every challenge—balancing execution excellence with a genuine belief that how we work together is as important as what we achieve.

www.linkedin.com/in/hilarygraham

13

THE QUIET WORK OF COURAGE

BY ANA RUELAS

*I*t was past our bedtime. The three of us sat midway up the stairs, peering curiously toward the kitchen below. Before I could even process what was happening, the sharp crack of a backhand echoed through the house. I froze. Then came my mom's voice, panicked, urgent, commanding.

"Run! Hide! Get under the bed! He's coming!"

I am the youngest of three. My brothers, Carlos and Juan, are five and six years older—Irish twins, close in age but different in spirit. Earlier that week, Carlos had opened a two-liter bottle of Pepsi that sat on the floor beside the refrigerator. When my father returned home that evening to refill his rum and soda, he discovered it had lost its fizz. He demanded to know who had opened it. As always, my mom took the blame.

Had she noticed earlier, she would have replaced it without question; anything to avoid conflict. But my father had come home ready for a fight—a fight he knew my mom would never win.

In his drunken rage, he stormed through the house toward the stairs as my mom shouted for us to hide. We darted up the stairs into the room we then shared and crawled under the beds, trembling.

My father, a man trained and uniformed by the National Guard, thundered after us, while my mom, who barely weighed one hundred pounds, tried to hold back a man nearly twice her size. We could hear the struggle, the sounds of desperation and love colliding in one terrible moment.

My mom had been raised to protect, to nurture. She was one of twelve—or maybe fourteen—siblings; even now, we laugh as we try to trace the exact number through ancestry records. Her childhood was one of survival through togetherness. They grew up with little, but what they had, they shared: rice stretched with love, laughter that covered the cracks of hard days, hands that reached out without being asked. Her siblings relied on one another, and that sense of collective care carried into everything she did. "If it happens to one, it happens to all," was their silent code—one my cousins and I still live by.

That unwritten promise became our family's language, spoken through gestures more than words—a meal left at the doorstep, a phone call made in the middle of the night, an extra bed always ready. When one of us aches, another somehow knows; when one succeeds, the others rise with pride. It is empathy in its truest form—not grand or performative, but steady, woven into the rhythm of our lives.

Even now, her family's side is scattered across cities and generations, carrying that same pulse of care. It's the comfort of knowing that somewhere, no matter what time or distance separates us, someone is saying your name in prayer, holding space for you in their heart. That is the legacy my mom and her siblings have instilled in us —not wealth or titles, but the certainty that love, when lived collectively, can keep even the most fragile family unbroken. A legacy I wish to pass on to my children.

My father's upbringing was the opposite. He had two half-siblings but was raised by a mom who was elegant, proud, and often cold. His father died young, and with that loss came a loneliness that shaped the edges of his life. Without the warmth of consistent affection, he learned early that survival depended on control, order, and proving himself.

Yet even in that solitude, he grew into a man of admirable qualities. He believed in discipline, in showing up on time, in doing things with precision. His work ethic was unwavering. He took pride in his appearance—his clothes neatly pressed, shoes polished, his hair always in place. There was a quiet dignity in how he carried himself, as though order and presentation could fill the space that tenderness had left behind.

My parents met in San Juan, Puerto Rico. They lived on parallel streets named Calle Luna and Calle Sol—Moon Street and Sun Street. It felt poetic then, and perhaps it was. They married young, had my brothers in quick succession, and built a life that swung between warmth and chaos.

Life with my father was complicated. We feared him, but we also admired him. There were moments of wonder—when his charm and humor filled the room, when he'd tell stories and jokes; with puzzles spread across the dining table, he'd share lessons in dominoes and pool and give talks about saving money and working hard. He was proud of his job at the *Municipio de San Juan* and his National Guard service. We were proud to help prepare his uniform, polish his boots, and make everything gleam just right. It made us feel close to him, part of something bigger than ourselves. For fleeting moments, he was gentle, almost luminous. He was our father. Yet, behind that structure and discipline lived a man still wrestling with the shadows of his own unmet tenderness.

But that night, everything changed.

In his rage, my father grabbed the wooden baton issued to him by the National Guard. Back then, batons were truly a masterpiece, made of a solid piece of wood covered in leather. He struck my mom, and her jaw fractured in two places. Then he went to sleep, still clutching the weapon like a trophy or perhaps a warning.

That night, my mom knew she needed medical care, but her fear of leaving us alone with him was stronger than the physical pain. The man who should have protected us had become the danger.

Still, my mom had her circle. This network of neighbors looked out for one another and for us. Our next-door neighbor, Angelita, a widow raising a child on her own, often took us in when my father turned us out. She'd make those nights feel like adventures, as though kindness could disguise fear. That night, my mom called her. Without hesitation, Angelita opened her door.

My mom lifted each of us over the low cement wall fence that divided our yards, handing her children into safety before seeking help for herself.

She couldn't drive; my father had forbidden it. It was another form of control. So, she called the neighbors across the street, who drove her to the hospital while her sister met her there.

I was too young to grasp time back then, but I know that after that night, everything began to shift. My mom chose to leave, trading fear for freedom, even if she didn't yet know how. She reached out to her family in New York City, who opened their doors, and soon after, we left.

The day we left, I remember us sitting in the back of a yellow taxi, watching our house as we drove away. My mom's tears fell silently until the cab driver, a stranger, spoke softly:

"*Señora, don't cry. You're doing the right thing. Everything will be okay.*"

I've never forgotten that moment and that man. His words were a small act of kindness—the kind that costs nothing but gives everything.

That day was the first, but not the last time, that my mom left my father. Deep down, my mom knew she needed a plan, not just an escape.

What I didn't know then was that courage rarely looks like what we imagine. It's not loud or cinematic; sometimes it's a woman carefully packing the essentials, praying her children will sleep through the sound of her heartbeat. It's the faith to believe that the smallest step toward safety is still progress.

That night planted the first seed of understanding that bravery and empathy are intertwined. My mom's love and compassion for us, even in her own terror, taught me that love will always find a way to move—if only an inch —toward light. When people ask me today where my drive comes from, I think back to her lifting us over the wall that night. It was more than escape; it was an act of creation. She was building a new story for us in real time.

Change did not arrive on our timeline, and survival often asks for compromises that look like detours. We returned home not long after leaving, caught between hope and habit. The house looked the same, but the air had shifted. I learned that leaving is sometimes a process, not a moment; a series of steps, not a single door.

Five years later, the sound of another slap pulled me from sleep. My brothers were now teenagers—fifteen and sixteen—and I was ten. We had moved two doors down to a bigger townhome so that I would have my own room. In those five years, my mom had gradually rebuilt herself. She earned her cosmetology license, learned to drive, took odd jobs—cutting hair, sewing, cooking, cleaning—anything to secretly save money. Our neighbors always found ways to keep her busy with those odd jobs to help her earn with pride and dignity.

That night, I heard my brother Carlos jump out of bed and the rapid, firm sound of his footsteps cutting through the dark as he marched toward my father. His voice was steady, fierce, and full of defiance as he spoke, "Why don't you hit a man instead of a woman!"

I ran to my bedroom doorway just in time to see my mom step between them, her small frame towered by these two men as she tried to make space and keep them apart, terrified my father might push my brother down the stairs. My father stared down at Carlos. "So," he said through clenched teeth, "you think you're a man now?" For a moment, the whole house seemed to hold its breath.

"Papi," I whispered from the doorway. My voice was small, but I wanted my father to see me. Even back then, I understood that daughters have a certain superpower when it comes to their fathers. My father turned back, looked at me, and walked back into his room.

My mom walked my brother back to his room, then came to mine. She kissed my forehead, tucked me in, and told me to go back to sleep. Her way of coping was always forward motion—to keep walking as though nothing had happened. It was survival disguised as strength. I think that's where I learned it too: when things are hard, the only way is forward.

The morning after that confrontation, the house was eerily quiet. The kind of silence that hums with things unsaid. My mom moved carefully, her body tense but her face calm—the same calm she wore whenever she was calculating what needed to happen next. She knew that what had happened between my father and Carlos had crossed a line that could not be mended. Carlos was growing into a young man, and my father's anger toward him frightened her in a new way. She needed to keep them both safe from each other.

She sat at the kitchen counter with the phone in her hand, staring at it for a long time before dialing. Her circle of care had always extended far beyond our neighborhood. It reached across cities, even across oceans of time and distance. That day, she called José and Josefina Marqués—dear friends who had known both my parents for nearly twenty years. José had once worked alongside my father in *El Municipio de San Juan*. After José retired, he and Josefina moved to Pompano Beach, Florida, with their three teenage children. They were like family to us.

When my mom's voice reached them across the line, they didn't hesitate. Josefina told her, "Send the boy. We'll take care of him until you can come." In that moment, I saw a kind of empathy that felt bigger than any act of charity—it was love in motion, immediate and certain. My mom trusted them completely.

She decided to send Carlos ahead, knowing that the tension between my father and him could ignite again at any moment. Her decision wasn't just about survival; it was about protection. She feared that Carlos's growing strength, and his fierce instinct to defend her, might push my brother or my father past the edge; and she feared what that would do to both of them.

The day Carlos left, my mom helped him pack a small suitcase—just a few clothes and other miscellaneous items. She held him for a long time. There were no dramatic goodbyes, just a gentle exchange of love and worry that only a mom and son can understand.

Soon after, we left my father for the second and final time. We left Puerto Rico with little more than a couple of suitcases and faith—carrying the invisible weight of hope. My brother Juan stayed behind with my aunt and uncle to finish his senior year of high school. Ten months later, after graduation, he joined us in Florida.

When we landed in Florida, José and Josefina were waiting—arms open, smiles warm, tears ready. Their kindness was simple yet profound, offering us a soft landing and a place to begin again.

Looking back, I see that my mom's choice to send Carlos ahead was an extraordinary act of empathy. It wasn't just about escaping danger; it was about choosing life for all of us. It was the hardest kind of love—the kind that sacrifices closeness for safety, comfort for peace.

We were safe.

The years that followed were not easy, but they were sacred in their own way—woven with the generosity of friends and strangers and the courage of my mom's steady rebuilding. Ours was a life patched together with borrowed strength and a community filled with people with similar struggles and open hearts.

Looking back, those years were my earliest education in what empathy feels like when it's lived, not simply spoken. It looked like my mom rising before the sun, making sure we were ready for school before heading to her sixteen-hour shift. It looked like my brothers working late at a gas station after school, handing their paychecks to help cover the rent for our tiny, one-bedroom, cockroach-infested apartment. It looked like me, at eleven years old, walking into an empty home, spending long hours alone—doing homework, cooking dinner for all of us, and eating by myself each night—while finding comfort in the cadence of responsibility. I learned self-trust in those years: how to cook rice without burning it, how to stretch groceries to make them last, and how to keep our little home clean, because dignity, I discovered, always begins there.

Our life was small but honest. I can still see us walking a couple of miles through the neighborhoods to reach the laundromat, our clothes and linens packed into black trash bags, my brother Carlos jogging ahead—training hard, chasing his dream of becoming a sports coach. Those moments, though humble and heavy, held a powerful kind of beauty. Within the hardship, we discovered the soft relief of peace. We were safe, we had harmony, and for the first time, a sense of stillness found us.

One December morning began like any other. We moved through our familiar routine—getting ready, gathering books, packing lunches. By then, my mom had saved enough to buy a small used car, a white Ford Pinto that felt like freedom on four wheels. My brother Juan, always the one responsible for getting everyone where they needed to be before starting his own long day, was already moving with purpose, ushering us out the door.

I headed to the bus stop with my classmate from across the street, while the three of them—my mom, Juan, and Carlos—climbed into the car and drove off. My mom and Juan went to work, and Carlos to school, wearing his usual smile—the kind that seemed to make the day brighter for everyone who crossed his path.

That morning, a friend of his had been crying at school. My brother, being who he was, couldn't ignore it. He learned that her mom was ill back in her home country and that she didn't have the money to help or even travel to see her.

After school, when Carlos arrived at the gas station to report for his shift, he asked for an hour off work to meet her. He didn't hesitate—he told her he would give her his paycheck. That was the kind of heart he had. Even at seventeen, he believed in showing up for people, not with words, but with action.

Every night followed a routine. My brother Juan would pick up my mom from her late-night shift at 11:15 p.m., then swing by the gas station to collect Carlos before heading home. They'd usually arrive a little before midnight. My mom would reheat dinner, they would eat, and get to bed to start again by 6 a.m.

But that night, everything shifted with one small, tragic choice. Because Carlos had taken that hour to help his friend, he stayed late to make it up. Not wanting to make everyone wait, he borrowed a friend's motorcycle, promising he would be home soon.

At 1:13 a.m., while driving across an intersection, a woman driving under the influence ran the light and struck him. My brother was killed instantly—pronounced dead on arrival.

Tragically, just a few days after my twelfth birthday, my brother Carlos was gone. It was devastating—then, now, and always.

That knock on our door still echoes through me. It was heavy, deliberate—the kind of sound that wakes you from sleep but freezes you where you stand. My mom opened the door, and in that instant when she saw José Marqués standing beside two detectives, she knew something had gone terribly wrong. She asked them to step in.

My brother Juan stepped forward, confusion already clouding his face. As soon as José saw him, he leaned in close and whispered the words that would change everything: "I didn't want to tell your mom, but your brother Carlos died."

Juan let out a raw, aching sound, a cry so deep it seemed to shake the walls around us. The detectives stood silently by the door, their faces marked by the heaviness of what they carried. It was clear they had done this before—delivered news that shatters lives—but there was still a sorrow in their eyes, the understanding of people who know there is no right way to break a heart.

My mom looked at them, her voice calm but trembling at the edges as she asked, "He died, didn't he?"

José closed his eyes, a tear slipping down his face as he nodded, confirming what words could not.

And in that instant, understanding washed over her. I watched her face collapse into a grief so profound it seemed to draw the air out of the room—the kind of grief that doesn't make a sound at first, just silence, then shaking, then the devastating unraveling of a world forever changed.

There are moments that divide your life into before and after—and that was ours. Grief does not ask for permission; it rearranges you. It is an ache that hurts all over. It lives in your chest, your bones, your breath. It's not just sorrow; it's the body remembering love and loss at the same time. With time, I realized it can also refine you—sanding away what is false, leaving what is true.

In the days that followed, the world kept moving as if nothing had happened, but we could feel time stop. Losing Carlos shattered something in all of us, but it also revealed something else—how empathy and love had defined him until his very last breath. His final act was one of generosity, of kindness extended without expectation. In many ways, he lived—and died—exactly as he was raised: giving, caring, believing that helping someone in need mattered more than anything else.

This is the legacy my mom instilled in my brothers and me, and I hope my children will carry it forward.

Even now, decades later, I think about the chain reaction of that single choice—to stop, to listen, to care—and how his spirit continues to remind me that empathy is not a concept. It's a way of being that extends beyond moments of crisis. It should exist in the everyday.

Losing my brother taught me lessons about empathy and love I did not realize I would need to support others later in life.

Growing up in a home shadowed by fear taught me that people often act from their own brokenness. My father's cruelty wasn't born of evil but of unhealed wounds, loneliness, and a desperate need to feel powerful in a world that once made him feel small.

It took years to understand that truth. Faith helped me forgive what I couldn't make sense of, and distance gave me the space to see my father not as the monster of my childhood, but as a man shaped—and perhaps shattered —by his own pain. Seeing him that way didn't excuse what happened; it simply widened my compassion until forgiveness felt possible.

Forgiveness came slowly, not in a single moment but through years of softening. I learned it isn't absolution— it's release. It's choosing peace over poison, reclaiming the energy that pain once consumed. When I finally forgave my father, I didn't condone his actions; I simply refused to carry his pain as my own. And when I asked for his forgiveness in return, I felt something I hadn't in years—lightness.

Empathy revealed itself most clearly in the moments that demanded courage—the ones that tested love in its purest form. When my mom was diagnosed with a brain tumor, I ran to her side. There were sleepless nights, long calls with doctors, and the fear that tried to take her voice but never her spirit. Even from afar, I held space for her strength, reminding her she wasn't walking that path alone.

It showed up again when my brother's health began to fail, as we found ourselves waiting—once more—for a kidney donor, suspended between hope and heartbreak. I ran to him too, to sit beside him, to listen, to reassure him that even in the waiting, love would hold him steady. Our circle widened as friends, neighbors, and family gathered with prayers and presence.

But empathy doesn't live only in the hard places—it's also in the joy of living. It also lives in the ordinary moments—in the rhythm of my days and the intentional ways we show up for one another. It's in the celebrations, big and small—the birthdays, the simple Sunday dinners where laughter fills the air, and in the silence I so deeply cherish. It's in the way friends lean in during happy and hard times, how we pause to truly see each other, how a single text or unexpected hug can remind someone they are held, seen, and loved.

It's in asking a stranger if they're okay and holding them just a second longer than expected—long enough for them to feel that someone cares. It's in the 10 a.m. call I make to my mom every day, our ritual of checking in—a small act that says, *I'm here. You're not alone.*

It's in the laughter of babies, the ease of shared stories, and the beauty and magic of watching our children speak with passion about what lights them up. It's dancing barefoot in the kitchen and watching the sunrise take our breath away.

It's the deep gratitude of mornings when everyone is safe, healthy, and home. It's in remembering to be present, even when life feels rushed—because love, like empathy, only exists in the moment you're in. It's the same current that has always moved through my life—from those early years of fear and survival to these years of peace and grace. The same force that once held us together now keeps me grounded and open to others.

My mom's lessons of empathy have made me a better human. They've turned pain into purpose, silence into strength, and fear into understanding. When I face setbacks, I think of her—moving forward even when her world was falling apart. I carry her courage like a map.

Resilience isn't about never breaking; it's about how you rise—softer, yet stronger—after you do. In the end, I return to the sound of my mom's steps moving through the dark—small, certain, enough. Her courage became our beginning. I think of her voice—steady, brave, and full of faith—whispering, *"Move forward."*

And that's the only way I know.

ANA RUELAS

Ana Ruelas is a leader known for building people and brands with purpose. She is the Founding and Managing Partner of The Agency Austin, a global luxury real estate brand recognized for its culture of collaboration and modern approach to service. Beyond real estate, Ana is a co-owner of Austin Woman Magazine, an organization dedicated to amplifying women's voices and stories through media and live events.

A former corporate executive with global experience at PepsiCo and Lenovo, Ana brings strategic vision, operational excellence, and a deep belief in purpose-driven leadership to every endeavor.

A longtime resident of Austin, she has built a portfolio of residential properties and investments across sectors such as healthcare, fintech, sports management, and consumer ventures. Yet, it's her community work that most reflects who she is at her core. Ana is deeply committed to causes that empower women and children, advance literacy, expand educational access, and support the arts. She has served in leadership and volunteer roles with organizations including Latinitas, Con Mi Madre, Texas Book Festival, Wonders & Worries, and Austin Symphony, among others.

Rooted in empathy and service, Ana's mission is to build community through connection, opportunity, and impact—creating spaces where people can thrive, belong, and dream big.

www.instagram.com/anaruelas713
www.linkedin.com/in/ana-ruelas0713
www.facebook.com/ruelasana
www.anaruelas.com

14

EMPATHY: MY PRACTICE, MY PRAYER, MY MEDICINE

BY ALICIA RAFFKIND

*W*hen I first walked through the doors of the treatment center, time stopped behaving. They took my phone, hairspray, and perfume. The clock didn't move forward; it looped back, forcing me to face everything I had been running from.

The intake nurse made me feel safe. The first night was a blur; my medication for my addiction kept me asleep for hours. I told myself I would just "get through" this, like serving a sentence. I didn't yet understand that getting clean wasn't a countdown. It was a reckoning.

In the common room the next morning, people greeted me with smiles and encouragement. That was the first kindness I noticed. The certainty in their voices helped me see myself again. Some days felt endless; others vanished without a trace. Mornings meant group sessions. Afternoons were for therapy. Evenings were quiet, filled with reflection. Beneath it all, empathy began to hum like a current that was quiet, invisible, and insistent.

In treatment, empathy was everywhere. It lived in how we sat together, holding each other up with small gestures, a shared silence, a moment of listening without trying to fix. Kindness can feel like a threat when you have lived on the edge for too long. Empathy doesn't announce itself. It seeps in. It fills the cracks where shame used to live.

I came into treatment thinking time would be my punishment. But as empathy began to ripple through the walls, in laughter that followed tears, time became something else. It became space. Space to breathe, to fall apart, to start again.

The walls had seen everything: the trembling first steps of detox, the whispered confessions, the anger, the laughter that came too soon and too loud. They didn't judge; they held it all.

Every morning at eight, we peeled back our layers in group therapy. The sameness of each day wore down my edges, the constant hum of humanity, the raw honesty of people with nothing left to hide. Something in me cracked open. Not all the way, just enough for the light to get in.

We sat with each other in the mess. We all carried our own weight of brokenness, but together we formed something almost holy, a community of the undone.

My perspective started to change, not just in the mirror, but in how I looked at others. My face softened. My voice was gentle. I found myself asking, "You okay?" and meaning it. I listened without interrupting, touched a stranger's shoulder without flinching, offered forgiveness without proof it would be returned.

By the time my recovery neared its end, the walls no longer felt heavy with suffering. They vibrated with something else, a collective heartbeat. We still laughed in the kitchen and cried in therapy, but we always found our way back to each other.

One night, during our final reflection circle, I said, "I learned that broken doesn't mean beyond repair, that laughter counts as prayer, and empathy grows even in places no one expects it." Everyone nodded. One woman wiped her eyes. For the first time, I wasn't performing recovery. I was living it.

Recovery changed us. It wasn't dramatic or cinematic. It was subtle, stubborn, alive. The kind of change that stays, the kind that follows you long after you leave the walls behind.

A sign of my continued recovery came when I was ready to give back. The day I walked through the women's shelter door, the women were stirring, getting ready for their day. The air smelled of coffee and disinfectant, the twin perfumes of survival. I had been sober long enough to trust my own hands again, but not long enough to forget what it felt like to be lost.

I told myself I came to volunteer to help. The truth was more complicated. I came because I needed to stand in a place where brokenness wasn't something to hide.

The women here reminded me of myself. Their faces were mirrors I needed to look into. They carried their stories like bags they couldn't set down. Some had been sleeping on benches. Some had children waiting somewhere. Some had mothers who had stopped answering the phone. Yet when they laughed, and they did, the sound was pure, like spring water breaking through stone.

The first time I sat with a woman four days into detox, she wept and trembled. Her face was red, her hands shaking. I wanted to say the right words, offer wisdom, and promise it would all be okay. None of that mattered. I held her hand instead and looked into her eyes, knowing I could never imagine everything she had seen.

One afternoon, a woman told me about her relapse and time in jail. She was angry at herself, her eyes heavy with shame. That moment shouldn't have mattered as much as it did, but in this place, warmth is holy.

The shelter is beautiful, with fresh paint, new mattresses, and green plants, but the women create the real beauty. They share shampoo, stories, cigarettes, and laughter. They speak their dreams in half sentences, afraid the words might vanish.

One bitter winter afternoon, they huddled under fuzzy blankets, humming gospel songs remembered from their grandmothers. The sound filled the room like heat. It didn't erase the cold. It built a fire inside it.

Then one woman relapsed and disappeared. The emptiness hit hard. A month later, she returned thinner, shakier, eyes downcast. "I messed up," she said. "Can I still come in?"

"Yes," we said. "Of course you can."

Empathy isn't clean. It's messy, cyclical, and exhausting. Sometimes it feels like holding a door open for someone you know might walk out again. But that's the point. You keep holding it open anyway.

Over the years, I have watched these women laugh, cry, and love each other fiercely. Kindness, I have learned, is rebellion. In a world that teaches us to guard ourselves and earn our worth, these women keep giving. A cigarette. A story. A hug that smells of cheap soap and courage.

When I drive home at night, the city hums around me.

Helping them hasn't made me stronger. It has made me softer. And in that softness, I have found strength.

The shelter can feel like a revolving door. Women come, stay for months, then vanish back into the world that bruised them. Sometimes they return, sometimes they don't. Their absence lingers, a forgotten coffee mug, a sweater left behind.

I used to think relapse was failure. When I was newly sober, I believed every slip erased your worth. Now I know relapse isn't the opposite of recovery. It is part of it, like the tide pulling back before it returns.

One afternoon, a woman told me she was pregnant. Her voice trembled with anger and shame. She had relapsed. A drink turned into three, then into a night she couldn't remember. The man was gone. No support. I listened without interrupting. Sometimes silence is the most merciful thing you can offer, the kind that doesn't judge or rush to comfort. Finally, I said, "You're here now. You're safe. That's what matters."

She didn't believe me. But she kept working, folding clothes, helping customers, fighting tears. Then she laughed at something a customer said, her shoulders relaxing. I winked at her, and she smiled back. That small moment gave me hope.

In my early days of sobriety, I used to flinch when others stumbled. I thought relapse was contagious. Now I know the opposite is true. When I see someone fall and rise again, I remember I can too.

Empathy isn't about saving anyone. It's about sitting close enough to someone's suffering that you remember your own humanity. It's about seeing the person, not the problem.

The women in the shelter tease each other, trade jokes, and cook meals together. The world outside may look away, but inside these walls, they are seen.

One morning, I woke up to a text: "Thank you for looking me in the eyes. No one has in a long time."

There's a saying in recovery: *we keep what we have by giving it away.* I used to think that meant sobriety. Now I know it means empathy.

When I leave the shelter, the city feels different. Not softer, but more honest. I see faces and wonder who they love, what they have lost, what keeps them up at night. I don't pity them. I notice them. That's what this place has taught me: to notice, to see, to listen.

Sometimes, when I get home, I sit in my car with the engine off, replaying the day, the laughter, the tears, the small mercies. I whisper a quiet thank you, not just for my sobriety, but for theirs, for the shared miracle of staying another day.

Pain, I have learned, can bring people together more powerfully than comfort ever could. The women here don't bond over what has gone right. They bond over the wreckage they are brave enough to lay bare. In that mess of confession and courage, kindness grows wild. It isn't polished or pretty. It shows up tired, trembling, and real.

There is something humbling about women rebuilding their lives from the ground up. They teach me that resilience isn't perfection. It's the willingness to begin again, over and over. They have become the heartbeat of this place, not saints, not martyrs, just humans doing the sacred work of surviving.

Empathy doesn't protect you from pain. It asks you to participate in it. To stay open, even when it hurts.

People ask why I keep coming back. I say, "Because you let me." The truth runs deeper. I come back because this place reminds me of what matters, the small things, the ordinary miracles. The laughter that bursts out of nowhere. The woman who starts to pray again, not for herself, but for someone else.

There is a quiet revolution here every day, though no one outside will write about it. It lives in small acts of care that multiply quietly, without permission.

Sobriety isn't just the absence of a substance. It's the presence of connection.

Empathy has become my practice, my prayer, my medicine.

One morning, under a pink sky, I felt something settle inside me. Kindness, no matter how small, keeps the world from falling apart. It isn't about saving anyone. It's about showing up again and again, even when all you have left is your presence.

The women in the shelter remind me daily that recovery isn't linear, empathy isn't neat, and love doesn't always look how we expect. Sometimes it's a song in the cold, a hand steadying another's shaking one.

Kindness doesn't fix everything, but it changes the air. It keeps hope alive.

When I lock the door and step into the night, I whisper the same words I once heard from a woman on her first day in recovery:

We're all just walking each other home.

And maybe that's the truest thing I know.

ALICIA RAFFKIND

Alicia Raffkind is a community leader and advocate in Amarillo, Texas, recognized by the Amarillo Globe News as a "Citizen on the Move" in 2022. For over two decades, she has dedicated herself to transforming lives through her work with the Downtown Women's Center (DWC), serving two terms as board president and helping raise millions of dollars for women seeking recovery from addiction.

Drawing from her own decade-long sobriety journey, Alicia combines her passion for fashion with her commitment to helping others through the DWC's Dress for Success program. As President of the DWC Ladies Auxiliary and a volunteer at the Uptown Shoppe, she empowers women to rebuild their lives with dignity and style.

Alicia serves on the Amarillo College Foundation Board and regularly speaks about recovery, hope, and personal transformation. Her mantra, "Keep on Keeping on," reflects her unwavering dedication to supporting women on their path to recovery and self-discovery.

15

THE QUEEN OF SHEBA

BY DANYELE EASTERHAUS

I'm sobbing in the back seat of our new soccer-mom van. My husband is in the driver's seat, frozen in grief. The August night presses in, thick, sticky, and relentless, as we sit on the third floor of the nearly empty hospital garage.

The air reeks of oil and exhaust. Overhead, yellow lights buzz and flicker, humming too loudly against the silence. Every so often, headlights slash across the concrete, lighting up half-faded graffiti. I fix my eyes on the bold shapes and colors while the tears spill down my cheeks.

We are both crying—raw, broken sobs that leave us gasping for air. Our hands swipe at our faces, as if we could wipe away what's far too heavy to hold.

In the middle of it all sits our most prayed-for gift: Brooke. She rests in the black car seat we picked out with hope, the one wrapped in baby-girl pink paper from Mom and Dad a few weeks earlier. She sleeps the way new babies do, heavy, like the whole world is safe.

This baby is everything we asked God for. The child we begged for by name. A dream come true wrapped in soft blankets. And yet... why does it all feel so wrong?

Why do the lights buzzing seem like they are screaming for me to move on? Why does joy carry such heavy sorrow? Because in giving us our miracle, someone else has lost theirs. That truth sits in my chest like a brick.

Ryan and I have been married for four years. I'm 38, Ryan is 33, and Paige is eight now. Life is good, and of course, we want more kids. We try and pray, but the tests are blunt: it isn't going to happen. My body simply can't carry another child.

Adoption felt obvious. Jeremy was just my brother. Not my "adopted brother," not "from another family." Just Jeremy. Adoption didn't change that—it never even crossed my mind. I thought adoption would be simple: want a baby, find a baby, adopt a baby. Life will be happy.

Turns out it isn't. It was beautiful and complicated, and man, it is layered with other people's pain in ways I could never imagine.

We gathered all our pictures, wrote a few notes, and started making a book that a potential birth family could look at to evaluate us. Our pale yellow adoption book was the "choose us" portion of the process. We smile out from a little rectangular window on the cover, the three of us vacationing and hiking in the Smokies. Beaming like we already belonged on the cover of someone else's story. On the top corner, in black Sharpie, our agency number, 2426, makes it official.

Inside this album, we tried to share the truth about ourselves through snapshots: our house, our dog, even the ridiculous cow-print chair that sat in the basement. The backyard, green and alive, with swings and toys scattered about. The three of us at the beach, salty hair and sunburned noses, laughing as we played in the waves and built lopsided sandcastles decorated with shells, joy holding it all together. We added notes about how we'd raise another child with our daughter. Every page whispered the same message: we're safe, we're fun, and we will love your baby.

Even while we viewed it together, I felt the ache in it. A birth mom, probably scared, probably exhausted, flipping through stacks of glossy strangers to decide who will raise her child. Hope and heartbreak in the same binder.

Then Brittany. Not a file or a number. She was a girl. Fourteen years old, with a baby growing inside of her while she was still in middle school, standing at the edge of decisions no child should ever have to face. Timid, yes, but also brave in ways she didn't even know yet.

She came into our lives not because we picked her, but because she picked us. Out of all the smiling pages, out of all the safe, staged stories, she looked at our pale-yellow book with our dog, our cow-print chair, Paige with her big-sister grin, and she said yes. She chose us.

Adoption isn't a lottery ticket. It isn't luck. It's someone, in one of the most difficult moments of their life, looking through books filled with strangers and deciding who will raise the child they already love. And Brittany, this quiet, scared, makeup-smudged teenager, looked at us and said: "Them!"

The first time I met her in person, I could barely breathe. She had this half-smile, part smirk and part armor, that reminded me of myself at fourteen. A little defiance, a little fear, and a lot of vulnerability. At that moment, I realized this wasn't just about a baby. It was about Brittany too.

She was so young, still giggling at silly things, trying on what it meant to be grown. But she was also carrying a life, carrying the weight of judgment, carrying more than her body or heart should have had to. And yet, in the middle of all that, she had made one of the most selfless choices a person can make.

Brittany chose us.

A week later, I picked up Brittany for her first prenatal check. She and her dad lived in a small, one-story house about forty-five minutes away. When I pulled in, a shiny black pickup sat in the driveway. She stepped out in red sweatpants and a blue side-tie shirt stretched over her belly, with a sleeveless denim shirt thrown over it. She looked so young, so small, and yet so very pregnant. My chest ached at the sight.

The clinic waiting room was dingy and cramped, the air thick with the smell of dust and old coffee. Chairs with cracked vinyl were smashed so close together that there was no space left for dignity, just knees bumping and eyes cast down. When the doctor finally came in, his presence carried no warmth. He was rude and dismissive, firing questions like accusations, his tone making it sound as if she had brought this on herself. He spoke over her, not to her, as though she were just a problem to be managed. It seemed as though he was scowling, the left side of his lip lifted high with utter disdain, as if to say, *Well, you got yourself into this situation.*

I was at my limit of kindness and asked the doctor to step into the hall. The fluorescent lights flickered above as I protectively explained that he would treat her with respect and speak only in kind words. "Treat her like the Queen of Sheba," I hissed, pulling my mother's line right out of my back pocket. "This is nonnegotiable." And yes, I poked his chest... pretty hard. Not exactly my proudest moment, but honestly, I'm not sorry.

I told him I'd be calling the director on my way home. People deserve dignity, especially kids in grown-up storms. The doctor stood with eyes wide and mouth agape. He apparently was able to take charge, call names, and be a jerk to most people, so he wasn't really sure how to act when I didn't allow it. Later, Brittany said no one had ever done that for her. No one had protected her. Her words cracked something open in me that I didn't even know was there.

As Brittany and I grew closer, questions around her pregnancy pressed in from every side. Doctors kept asking, "Do you know when you got pregnant?" Every time, she gave the same answer: "I don't know." And then Brittany asked me, "Why can't the doctors tell me?"

At first, I thought it was simple confusion. But slowly, I heard the deeper truth: she didn't have the pieces to make sense of what had happened. What Brittany had couldn't be called memory, but small shards and wreckage: waking to confusion, hours missing, boys surrounding her, something taken from her she couldn't put into words.

When she tried to tell an adult, she was told flatly, "That didn't happen. You're stupid."

I can't imagine being thirteen, finally speaking the most frightening words you can form, only to have your reality erased in a single sentence. She learned to disappear.

I felt a heat rise up that I barely recognized, a kind of righteous anger. I wasn't her family, but I could be her witness. I could ask the questions, name the wrongs, give her the language she'd been denied. My own thirteen-year-old self stirred, remembering the version of me who had been taken advantage of and told her story wasn't hers to tell. This time, I wouldn't be quiet.

We began building a relationship and trust. We did ordinary things together once a week. We had appointments, but mostly we ate Rally's cheese fries, Taco Bell nachos, and drank Mountain Dew and pink lemonade in the biggest size they sold. We walked in malls without buying anything, giggling and trying on clothes. We even watched a few movies to borrow a life that wasn't ours for a couple of hours. People assumed I was her mom.

In those small booths and long walks, we built trust. We also started naming boundaries—or I did, as she was just learning what they were. What did she need as a birth mom? What did we need as adoptive parents? I was not there to replace her mother. That wound wasn't mine to step into. I was there to care for the girl in front of me and the baby growing at turbo speed inside her. We weren't a typical family, but love was cementing something fierce and unusual between us. To pull out a word from Stitch, an *ohana*, long before any judge or paper said so.

By late summer, she called herself a "walking blimp." Nothing fit her young, swollen belly. Her face and hands began to swell, but not as much as her poor feet. August heat in Indiana is rude; in a fourteen-year-old body carrying a full-term baby, it's an oven. Brooke seemed content to live in utero forever. But she was getting huge, so the doctor scheduled an induction.

Adoption rules and attorneys turn what should be a joyful time into something measured and restrained. No one from our side of the family was allowed at the hospital. Paige took it like a champ—sad, but shining at the thought of becoming a big sister. My parents were gutted, though they understood. We all knew the rules, and we honored them, holding our excitement quietly, the way you do when love isn't allowed to show.

When the day came, Brittany wanted to be with people she trusted. So it was my husband, me, and her sister in the delivery room. We'd done all the classes together—breathing, positions, all the pre-game. We were ready, but also, you're never prepared.

The hospital room pulsed with heat and fear, some named fears, but mostly unspoken ones. Brittany, drenched in August sweat and fluorescent light, tried to smile, but exhaustion hollowed her face. She was still a child, about to give birth to another.

Her sister clutched one hand. I gripped the other, whispering encouragement, counting each ragged breath. Ryan stood at the head of the bed, a cool cloth always ready. That was his role—steady, practical, giving her small mercy when the contractions threatened to crush her.

Thirty-six hours in, Brittany's body trembled with every push. Too young. Too small. The monitors beeped sharper, faster. Brooke's oxygen was slipping.

The hospital staff swarmed around, their voices clipped and cold. Then came the word nobody wanted to hear: *C-section.* For a girl this young, it wasn't just a surgery; it could mean no more children. For what someone else had done, she'd be the one paying. So we did the only thing we could at that moment: we prayed.

In a brief moment of quiet, Brittany resting between contractions, I pulled out my phone and typed: pray for strength for Britt and for her safety. The text flew off to the people who knew us, who knew what Brittany was carrying. The room filled with so many angels I could feel their wings brushing my cheeks. They were there to protect Brittany and to usher Brooke safely into the world. It gave me peace, knowing God had brought us here, and He would take us through it. And then the young, sweet doctor said, "Here's the baby."

Brittany pushed with the last scraps of strength her body had. And then came Brooke—nearly nine pounds and twenty-two inches of fierce life. She was there, in flesh, and I could hardly catch my breath long enough to understand what had just happened. She was born silent, meconium-stained, and danger was thick in the air. The respiratory team swarmed in to ensure they could clear her lungs. A surgical team stood outside, ready to wheel Brittany away just in case. The silence was brutal and deafening. Seconds dragged on as we stood there, frozen, afraid to breathe.

A single roar rose through the room, unyielding and alive, carrying with it the relief of knowing life was here and refused to be quiet.

I stood there stunned. Brooke was in flesh, beauty from ashes. Something so horrid had brought her into this world, and there was only great bounding, beauty, and love in her. I glanced around for Ryan and couldn't find him. Then I saw his feet beyond the curtain, just outside the door. He was on the floor, face in his hands, red-faced and sobbing. He looked up, eyes wet. "She's the most beautiful thing I've ever seen." That was the moment I watched a man become a new dad. That man would never be more attractive than that very moment.

Brittany, Ryan, and I had chosen her name together: Brooke Ashlyn. "B" for Brittany, "lyn" from Brittany's middle name. A little thread tying them always, even if they didn't live in the same house.

We stayed the week. We taught and learned and stared. Brittany was bright-eyed and brave, soaking up all the things of babies: diapers, burping, bottle angles, and "Is this normal?" I sat beside her and taught as much as she wanted to learn, both of us aware that this part would soon come to an end.

On paperwork day, they led us into separate rooms, which felt so clinical, sterile, and designed to keep us apart. It felt wrong. After everything we had shared, Brittany and I should have been side by side. Instead, she was in one room, and I was in another, each of us holding pens that would change our lives.

Indiana doesn't recognize open adoption, keeping identities and contact completely confidential—even when everyone involved longs for it. The system has its own voice. So we signed. She signed. Witnesses stood by. A judge's approval would come later.

The process was cold, almost mechanical, and it broke something in me. How could something so holy— sacrifice, love, the passing of a child from one set of arms to another—be reduced to paperwork and signatures? It felt stripped of humanity, like somebody had boiled down the life we lived together for months into a stack of legal forms.

Leaving the hospital gutted us. No one warned us what it would feel like—walking out with a newborn while her birth mother stayed behind, empty-armed. Legal or not, it felt unbearable. We loved Brittany. We loved Brooke. And still, we were leaving one to grieve while we carried the other home.

By the time we reached the van, we collapsed. Sobs like a flood, unstoppable. How could love hold so much joy and so much grief at once? It was the universe split in two—good and hard colliding.

Days turned into weeks, weeks into months—and then came the day of our first visit to the Adoption Support Center, where Brittany would see Brooke again for the first time. Walking in, my stomach was in knots. It was so unnerving. *What if it felt weird? What if it wasn't as good as we hoped? What if Brooke squirmed away, or cried, or didn't want to be with the girl who had carried her?* The questions wouldn't stop circling.

Brittany came with her dad. He was quiet at first, but his eyes gave him away. He was smitten the moment he saw Brooke. There was grief there too, raw and honest, because he had already lost the chance to see his granddaughter every day as she grew. But even in the ache, you could see the love spilling over. He adored Brittany, and in an instant, that same love transferred to Brooke. They even shared the same smile, wide and warm, and when they both grinned at her, it was as if the line of family stretched across generations right in front of me.

Paige hovered close to my side. She had her little pageboy haircut, blonde hair framing her face, and those big brown eyes that made her look like a Precious Moments doll. She was absolutely smitten, so proud to be Brooke's big sister, and equally delighted that Brittany felt more like a sister to her than anything else. There were only six years between them, after all. They teased and giggled like siblings, and it softened the edges of tension in the room. This visit wasn't just between "birth mom" and "adoptive family." It was a tangle of sisters, each claiming a piece of belonging.

Brittany wore bright blue eyeshadow brushed heavily across her eyelids. It struck me in an instant—of course she did. She was fourteen. She was still a kid who wanted to play with makeup and feel grown-up, even as she carried the weight of choices most adults never face. That eyeshadow said everything: underneath the layers of strength and sacrifice, she was just a girl.

I'll never forget the look on Brittany's face when she saw Brooke. It was like staring into a living mirror. The same wide-set eyes. The same tiny button nose. We laughed together when we saw they had the same little square, Fred Flintstone feet. When Brooke fell asleep, her head tilted at that strange angle Brittany had as a teenager, and it nearly broke me. Genetics is fundamental, and it's holy in its own way.

When I handed Brooke over, my hands hesitated—half protective, half trembling with the weight of it. But Brooke, true to form, was never one to sit still. She wiggled and squirmed, craning her neck to see the room, her little arms pushing to be free. She was a mover and shaker from the very beginning, just like her birth mom. Brittany laughed through her nerves, shifting Brooke from side to side, trying to keep up with the tiny bundle who had no interest in being cradled. The similarity was uncanny; both of them are restless, full of energy, unwilling to be contained.

We chatted about school, about Paige's activities, about small things that didn't matter, but underneath, I could hear my own pulse thudding in my ears. I kept watching Brittany's dad. He leaned forward when Brooke made the slightest sound, his whole body bending toward her like she was sunlight. Loss and pride mingled in his face, and it struck me hard: adoption never severs love. It only changes the way love looks.

That first visit was awkward. Tender. Sacred. It felt like walking on holy ground, where joy and grief were both thick in the air. But over the years, we slowly became family—not legally, not in a picture-perfect way, but in the gritty, real-life sense. Brittany began calling me "Momma D." I called her Britt, and sometimes "my girl," because that's what she felt like to me. She wasn't a project or a problem; she was part of us.

Britt went on to graduate high school—the very first in her family to do so. And our family erupted in cheers, tears, clapping. We made it a celebration because milestones like that deserve to be marked. God had taken a scared thirteen-year-old who didn't know where to turn and written a new story.

She didn't follow the traditional path people expect, with college, a career, and tidy next steps. But she kept moving forward, finding her way, building a life, and eventually becoming a mother again. Her road hasn't been easy, but we've walked it side by side—through moves, cars, hospitals, and hard choices. Showing up isn't optional. It's who we are.

She watched Brooke graduate from high school, cheered as she went on to earn her certifications in welding school. Through it all, Brittany was her biggest cheerleader, the one in the background saying, "Don't ask me, ask your mom. That's her job." There was even a season, after Brittany's first son was born, when she and the baby lived with us for about three months. The basement bedroom became hers, and for the first time, we could be on-site to teach her the parenting skills she hadn't gotten the chance to learn with Brooke. It was a full circle, watching her mother, correcting when needed, and giving her breaks when the overwhelm pressed in. She did well. And when the time was right, with boundaries in place, she moved forward and carried her life with her. It was messy and brave and exactly what growth looks like. Brittany is raising her boys with grit and love, rewriting a family line in ways that echo far beyond her knowledge. Every homework assignment finished, every bedtime story read, every "I love you" whispered is a kind of generational healing. She may not always see it, but I do, and God is still writing through her.

Brooke is everything I never knew I needed to learn—grit and grace wrapped in one wild, determined soul. She's fierce and funny, a fighter who doesn't understand stop. She took her driver's test sixteen times before passing on the seventeenth, and she laughed the whole way through. That's who she is—tenacious, light-filled, unshakably kind. She carries Brittany's fire and my steadiness, somehow making them her own. She loves wide, forgives quickly, and stands tall in a world that once told her she might not belong. She's living proof that beauty can rise from ashes, that love can build where pain once stood.

And as for me, I carry both Brittany and Brooke with me into every room I enter. Into my work, into leadership, and into conversations with people who feel unseen. Because once you've held the hands of a scared teenager in labor, and once you've walked out of a hospital sobbing because joy and grief shared the same breath, you don't see people the same way. You see them as people, not problems.

The future isn't neat. It's not tied with a bow. It will be messy. It will be beautiful. It will be both. Life layered with both grief and joy, just like that August night in the hospital garage. Beauty comes in the overlap. That love and loss can live in the same breath. But if this story has taught me anything, it's that God is faithful in the middle. He doesn't just write endings—He writes next chapters. And He writes them through people who never thought they'd be part of the story.

That's what I believe for Brittany. That's what I believe for Brooke. And that's what I believe for me. This story may be ours, but it's also a mirror. A reminder that every face you pass belongs to someone with a story. Everyone —*everyone*—is worth dignity.

So I keep showing up for Brittany and for Brooke. For the boys and for the people God keeps placing in my path. Because everyone deserves to be seen, heard, and loved. Because sometimes, out of the hardest places, God gives you a glimpse of forever. Sometimes, you end up with a Brooke.

DANYELE EASTERHAUS

Danyele Easterhaus is an entrepreneur, writer, and speaker who believes every person—no matter their story —deserves to be seen, felt, heard, and loved. She is the founder of Danyele Easterhaus Consulting, where she equips mission-driven leaders to create cultures of belonging and lead with authenticity.

Her perspective is shaped by decades of nonprofit leadership and her family's journey through adoption, parenting, and fostering. Alongside her husband, Ryan— affectionately known as "Hot Hubs"—she has raised four daughters, has fostered 11 other children, and continues to advocate as a GAL in the court system, fighting for the best interests of kids who no longer have a voice in DCS. With lived experience that includes parenting a daughter on the autism spectrum and another navigating mental health and borderline personality disorder, Danyele writes and speaks from the messy middle of real life, reminding others that leadership, like family, is never perfect but always worth showing up for.

www.danyeleeasterhausconsulting.com
www.facebook.com/danyele.easterhaus
www.linkedin.com/company/danyele-easterhaus-consulting

OUR NON-PROFIT PARTNERS

Spread the love!

All proceeds from our multi-author books are donated to a nonprofit organization making a meaningful difference in the lives of women or children in Austin, Texas, where Sulit Press is headquartered.

By purchasing this book, you're not only supporting the voices and stories of the women who contributed—you're also helping fund real change in the local community.

We periodically select new nonprofit partners to ensure that the impact of each book continues to reach where it's needed most.

To learn more about our current partner organization, please visit our website at www.sulitpress.com.

Ready to fast-track your publishing career, increase your visibility, or boost your business?

If this book is in your hands, chances are you've got something powerful to say, too.

At Sulit Press, we help women write just one chapter that opens doors—whether that's to new clients, speaking gigs, media features, or simply the joy of finally being published.

By contributing to a multi-author book, you'll gain:

- A clear and supported path to becoming a published author
- Visibility for your work, business, or message
- A powerful network of fellow authors and creatives

This is for you if:

✅ You're passionate about what you do and ready to share it

✅ You're committed to showing up and doing your best work

✅ You're excited to be part of something bigger

Ready to explore what's possible?

Visit sulitpress.com to learn how you can get published, join a powerful community, and grow your visibility.

www.ingramcontent.com/pod-product-compliance
Lightning Source LLC
Chambersburg PA
CBHW021218130626
46554CB00004B/1257